TABLE OF CONTENTS

	Page
Tuning the Banjo	4
Basic Musical Knowledge	5
Tablature	8
Major Chord Forms	9
Dominant 7th Chord Forms	10
Key of C Major	11
Non-chordal Tones in C Major	16
Key of A Minor	18
Minor Chord Forms	19
Harmonizing Non-chordal Tones in A Minor	22
Key of G	24
Harmonizing Non-chordal Tones in G	27
Key of E Minor	29
Harmonizing Non-chordal Tones in E Minor	32
Key of F	33
Harmonizing Non-chordal Tones in Key of F	35
Key of D Minor	37
Harmonizing Non-chordal Tones in D Minor	39
Diminished Chords	41
The Augmented Chord	43
Key of B Flat	45
Harmonizing Non-chordal Tones in B Flat	47
Key of G Minor	49
Key of D Major	51
Harmonizing Non-chordal Tones in D Major	53
Key of B Minor	55
Harmonizing Non-chordal Tones in B Minor	57
Key of E Flat	58
Harmonizing Non-chordal Tones in E Flat	60
Key of C Minor	61
Harmonizing Non-chordal Tones in C Minor	63
Key of A Major	64
Harmonizing Non-chordal Tones in Key of A Major	66
Key of F Sharp Minor	68
Key of A Flat	71
Non-chordal Tones in Key of A Flat	73
Key of F Minor	74
Harmonizing Non-chordal Tones in F Minor	76
Key of E Major	77
Non-chordal Tones in Key of E	79
Key of C Sharp Minor	80
Harmonizing Non-chordal Tones in C Sharp Minor	82
Key of D Flat Major	83
Harmonizing Non-chordal Tones in D Flat	85
Key of B Flat Minor	86
Key of B Major	88
Key of G Sharp Minor	90
F Sharp/G Flat Major	92
E Flat/D Sharp Minor	94
Major 6th Chords	96
Minor 6th Chords	99
Major 7th Chords	101
Minor 7th Chords	103
7th Augmented 5th Chords	106
7th Diminished 5th Chords	108
9th Chords	110
Altered 9th Chords	113
11th Chords	114
13th Chords	116

The Correct Way to Hold the Tenor Banjo

Practice holding the Tenor Banjo in this manner.

Keep the palm of the hand away from the neck of the instrument.

The Left Hand

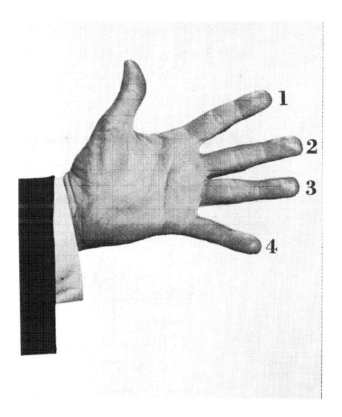

Striking the Strings

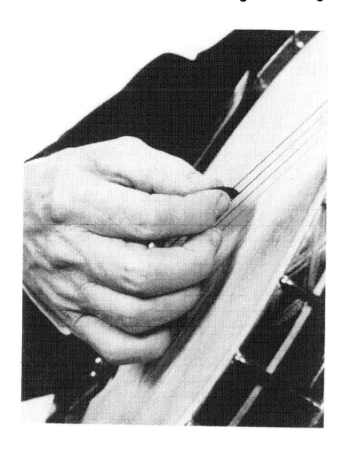

This is the Pick

Hold it in this manner ⟶ firmly between the thumb and first finger. Use a medium soft pick.

Turning the Tenor Banjo

First String .... **A** ①
Second String .... **D** ②
Third String .... **G** ③
Fourth String .... **C** ④

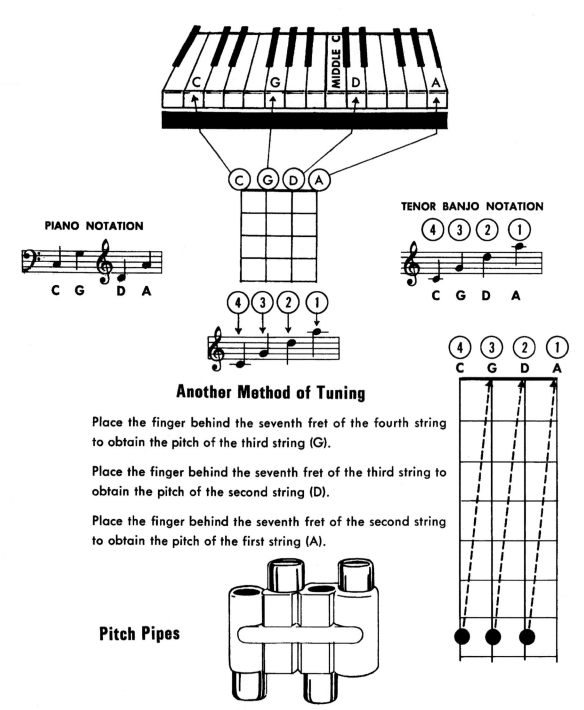

Another Method of Tuning

Place the finger behind the seventh fret of the fourth string to obtain the pitch of the third string (G).

Place the finger behind the seventh fret of the third string to obtain the pitch of the second string (D).

Place the finger behind the seventh fret of the second string to obtain the pitch of the first string (A).

Pitch Pipes

Pitch pipes for the Tenor Banjo (Cello) may be purchased at any music store. Each pipe will have the correct pitch of each Tenor Banjo string. These are an excellent investment.

The Rudiments of Music

The Staff

Music is written on a STAFF consisting of FIVE LINES and FOUR SPACES.

The lines and spaces are numbered upward as shown:

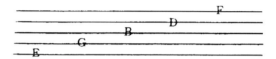

They also have LETTER names.

The LINES are named as follows: 1-E, 2-G, 3-B, 4-D, 5-F.

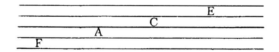

The letters can easily be remembered by the sentence —

Every Good Boy Does Fine.

The letter-names of the SPACES are: 1-F, 2-A, 3-C, 4-E.

They spell the word **F-A-C-E**.

The musical alphabet has seven letters — A, B, C, D, E, F, G.

The Clef

This sign is the TREBLE or G CLEF

All Banjo music will be written in this clef.

The STAFF is divided into MEASURES by vertical lines called BARS.

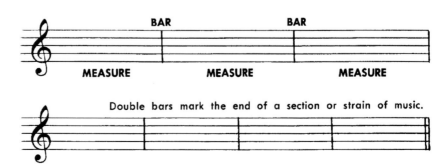

Double bars mark the end of a section or strain of music.

5

Notes

THIS IS A NOTE:

A note has three parts.

They are — the HEAD ●, the STEM |, and the FLAG ♪

NOTES MAY BE PLACED IN THE STAFF,

BELOW THE STAFF,

AND ABOVE THE STAFF.

A note will bear the name of the line or space it occupies on the staff.

The location of a note in, above or below the staff will indicate the Pitch.

PITCH: the highness or lowness of a tone.   TONE: a musical sound.

o	This is a WHOLE NOTE The head is hollow. It does not have a stem.	♩ (half)	This is a HALF NOTE The head is hollow. It has a stem.
♩	This is a QUARTER NOTE The head is solid. It has a stem.	♪	This is an EIGHTH NOTE The head is solid. It has a stem and a flag.

Note Values

o = 4 BEATS	A WHOLE-NOTE will receive Four Beats or Counts.	♩ = 2 BEATS	A HALF-NOTE will receive Two Beats or Counts.
♩ = 1 BEAT	A QUARTER NOTE will receive One Beat or Count.	♪ = ½ BEAT	An EIGHTH-NOTE will receive One-half Beat or Count. (2 for 1 beat)

Rests

A REST is a sign used to designate a period of silence.

This period of silence will be of the same duration of time as the note to which it corresponds.

This is a WHOLE REST ▬ Note that it hangs DOWN from the line.	This is a HALF REST ▬ Note that it lays ON the line.	This is a QUARTER REST 𝄽
		This is an EIGHTH REST 𝄾

Notes and Comparative Rests

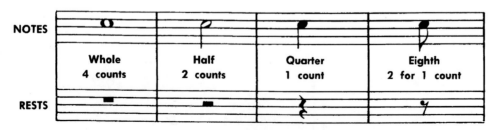

The Time Signature

  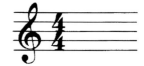

The above examples are the common types of time signatures to be used in this book.

> $\frac{4}{4}$ - THE TOP NUMBER INDICATES THE NUMBER OF BEATS PER MEASURE.
> $\frac{4}{4}$ - THE BOTTOM NUMBER INDICATES THE TYPE OF NOTE RECEIVING ONE BEAT.
> $\frac{4}{4}$ TIME AND COMMON-TIME ARE THE SAME.
>
>   4 - BEATS PER MEASURE.
>   4 - A QUARTER-NOTE RECEIVES ONE BEAT.

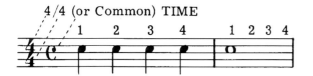

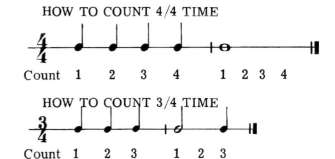

Ledger Lines

When the pitch of a musical sound is below or above the staff, the notes are then placed on, or between, extra lines called LEDGER LINES.

> The music is to be played one octave higher than the written music. The sign indicating this is 8va.
>
> Playing an octave higher than the written music will enable the banjoist to play directly from the vocal line of the popular and standard song sheets in true melody chord style.

PLAY 8VA
EXAMPLE
Play this line:

REMEMBER - ALL Music to be Played 8va
(One Octave Higher than written)

The Tenor — Banjo Fingerboard

Reading Upward The Strings Will Be Numbered ④ ③ ② ①

④ — Largest string.   ① — Smallest string.

The encircled numbers ④ ③ ② ① will be the numbers of the STRINGS.

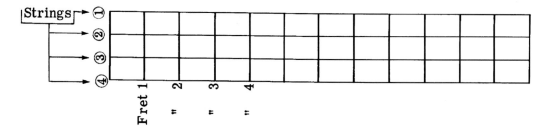

The Tablature

The horizontal lines are the BANJO STRINGS.
The number on each STRING indicates FRET LOCATION.
The number in parenthesis ( ) indicates LEFT HAND FINGER.
The encircled number ◯ at the head of the Tablature indicates the number of the string.
⊗ = String not played.

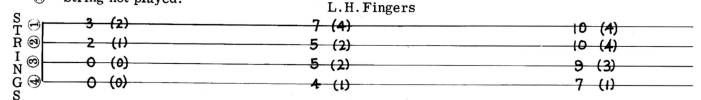

The horizontal lines are the strings.   The vertical lines lines are the frets.

Actual Pitch *8va*

When the pitch places a note so high above the staff that reading becomes difficult the notation may be lowered one octave. This is "Actual Pitch" in Tenor Banjo music. The term *8va* is used for this.

"Loco" means return back to the orginal notation.
The notes on the first string in Actual Pitch.

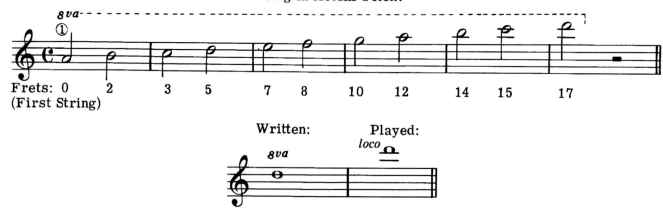

8

The Major Chord Forms

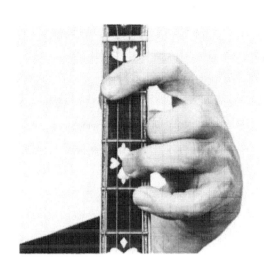

Form I

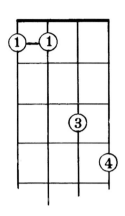

Form III

Form V

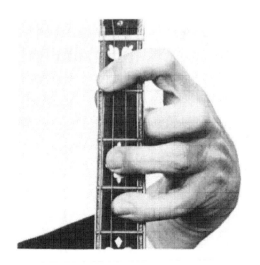

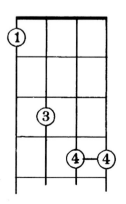

The Seventh Chord Forms

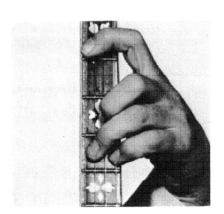

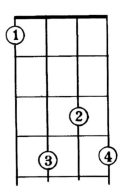
Form I7

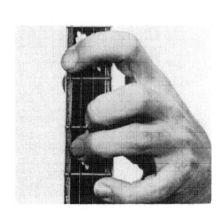

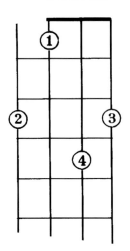
Form III7

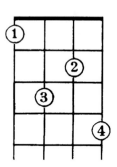
Form V7

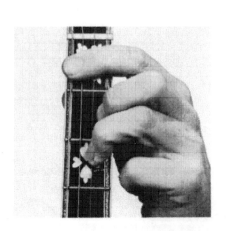

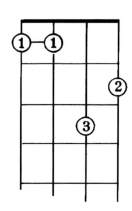
Form VII7

The Chords In The Key Of C

The Chords in The Key of C Are: C, F, & G7

Practice The Following Chord Studies in This Manner:

1 - One strum per chord. Strum slowly in a harplike fashion. (⁞ = Harplike).
2 - Strum each chord four times on the whole-notes and two strums for each half-note.

o = / / / /   𝅗𝅥 = / /   A quarter note will receive one strum.   ♩ = /

3 - Pick the melody note as a single note followed by three strums for the whole-notes and one single note followed by one strum for each half-note.

X = single note   o = X / / /   𝅗𝅥 = X /

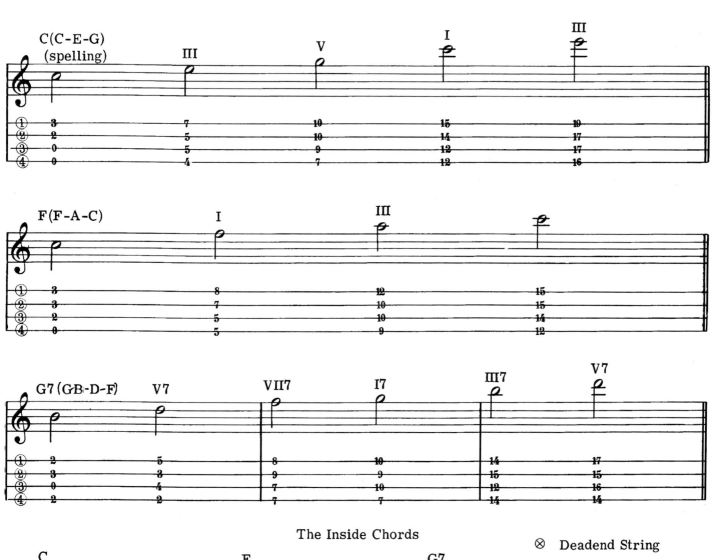

The Inside Chords

⊗ Deadend String

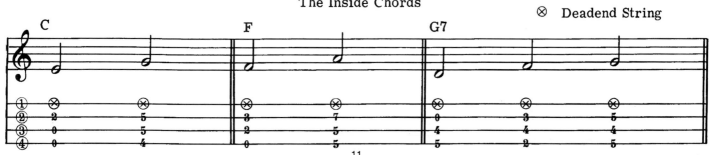

Chord Study In The Key Of C

The Harmonized Scale

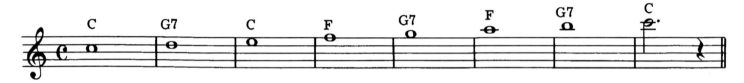

Chord Etude

Our First Solo

C = Common Time

Mel Bay

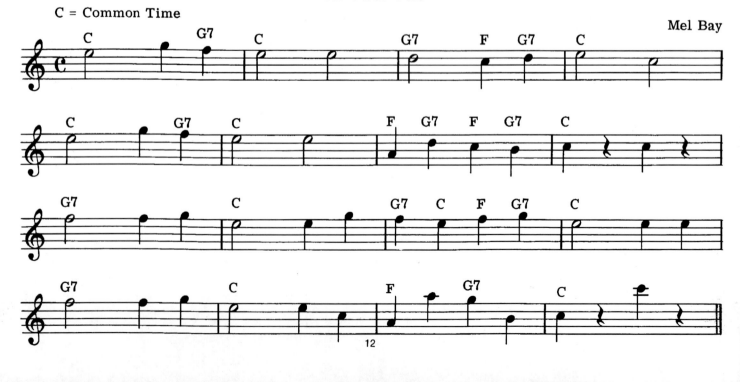

Three—Four Time

THIS SIGN  INDICATES THREE-FOUR TIME

3 – Beats Per Measure
4 – Type of Note Receiving One Beat
(Quarter-Note)

In three-four time, we will have three beats per measure.
A quarter note will receive one beat.

Dotted
Half Notes

A dot (·) placed behind a note increases its value by one-half.
A dotted half-note (𝅗𝅥.) will receive three beats.

The Tie

The TIE is a curved line between two notes of the same pitch.
The first note is played and held for the time duration of both.
The second note is not played but held.

Example

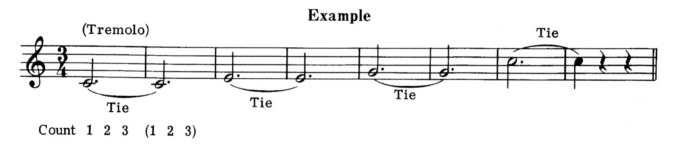

Count 1 2 3   (1 2 3)

Down In The Valley

The Notes On The Third And Second String
(Actual Pitch)

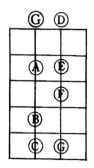

In most melodies, the notes on the third string will be played as single notes.
(X)

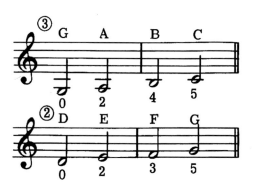

The Tremolo

At this time we should start the development of the tremolo.

The tremolo is a very rapid down and up stroking of the pick giving a sustained tone. The tremolo will be employed on all notes receiving more than two beats. The sign for tremolo is 𝄋

Study

Old Black Joe

The Chordal Tones

Chordal tones belong to the structure of the chord.

The Major chord construction consists of the root, third and fifth notes of the Major Scale. (1st, 3rd and 5th) This explains the naming of the chord forms Form I, Form III and Form V. The TOPNOTE or MELODY NOTE will be as named in the form number.

example:

Theoretical construction and concept will be bypassed. In order to facilitate melody chord playing, only basic theory will be employed. A complete course in theory and harmony is recommended as a supplement to this book or as a follow up for good musicianship.

Seeing Nellie Home

The Non Chordal Tones

A Non-Chordal tone is a tone not belonging to the chord.
As explained above, the C chord contains the following notes: C-E-G.
All other notes in the C scale are Non-Chordal. (Not a part of the chord)

In the example note that the chordal tones are designated I, III and V, The Non-Chordal tones will be in parenthesis.

The tones Non-Chordal to the C chord are D, F, A and B.

Harmonizing a Non-Chordal tone will be done in this manner:
1. Place the Major form nearest to the Non-Chordal tone.
2. Substitute the top-note with the Non-Chordal tone leaving the remaining portion of the chord undisturbed. In other words, the chordal top-note will be replaced by the Non-Chordal top-note.

Harmonizing The Non—Chordal Tones With The C Chord

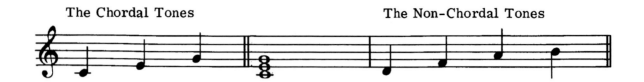

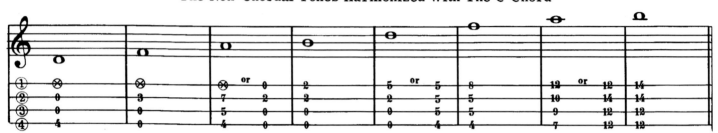

Harmonizing The Non—Chordal Tones With The F Chord

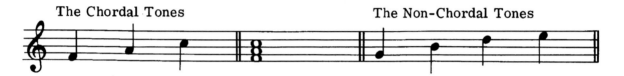

Harmonizing The Non—Chordal Tones With The G7 Chord

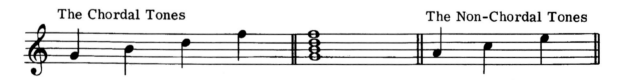

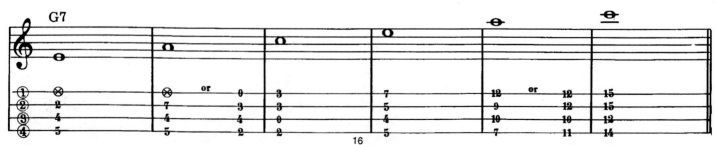

Two Optional Seventh Chord Forms

A Study Harmonizing Chordal And Non—Chordal Tones

The non-chordal tones will be indicated in this manner ( ).

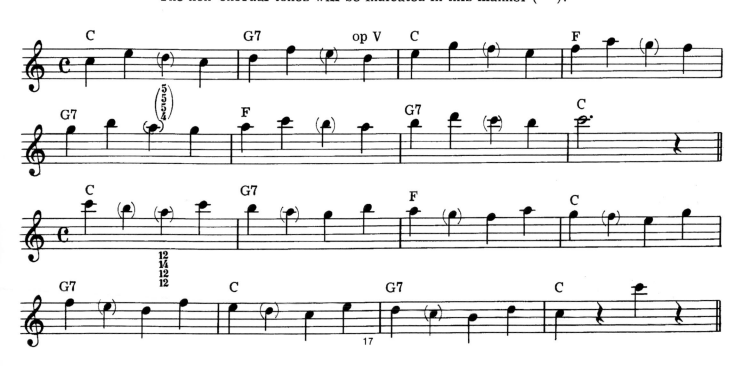

Steps

A Half-Step is the distance from a given tone to the next higher or lower tone. On the Banjo the distance of a Half-Step is ONE FRET.
The distance of a Whole-Step on the Banjo is TWO FRETS.
The C Scale has two half-steps. They are between E-F and B-C.

The Key Of C

All music studied so far in this book has been in the Key of C.
That means that the notes have been taken from the C Scale (shown below) and made into melodies.
It is called the C Scale because the first note is C and we proceed through the musical alphabet until C reappears. C-D-E-F-G-A-B-C.
We will cover the subject of keys and scales more thoroughly in the Theory and Harmony Chapters appearing later on in this course.
At present we will deal only with basic fundamentals.

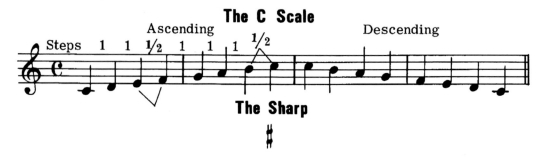

The Sharp

The SHARP placed before a note raises its pitch 1/2-step or one fret.

The Flat

The FLAT placed before a note lowers its pitch 1/2-step or one fret.

The Natural

The NATURAL restores a note to its normal position. It cancels all accidentals previously used.

The Key Of A Minor

(Relative to C Major)

Each Major key will have a Relative Minor key.
The Relative Minor Scale is built upon the *Sixth tone* of the Major Scale.
The difference between the two scales is the arrangement of the Whole-Steps and Half-Steps.

Harmonic

The 7th tone is raised one Half-Step ascending and descending.

Melodic

The 6th and 7th tones are raised one half-step ascending and lowered back to their normal pitch descending.

The Minor Chord Forms

Minor Form Im

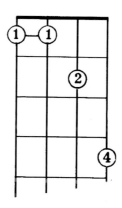

Minor Forms IIm

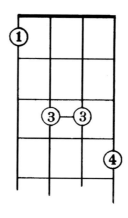

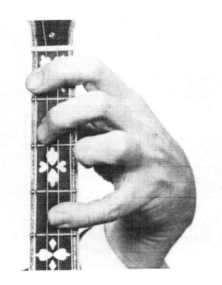

Minor Form Vm

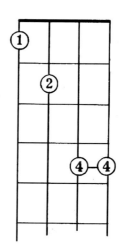

The Chords In The Key Of A Minor

The Chords in The Key of A Minor Are : Am, Dm & E7.

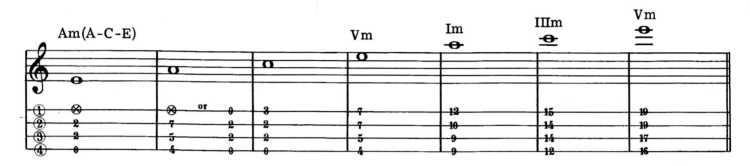

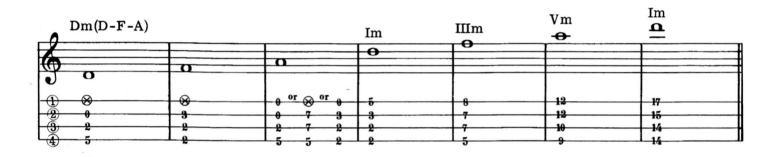

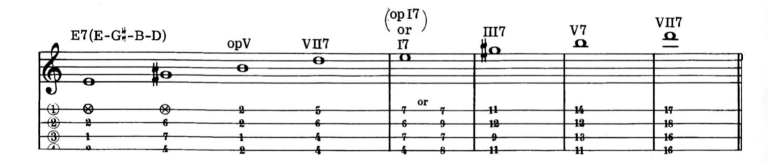

A Chord Study In A Minor

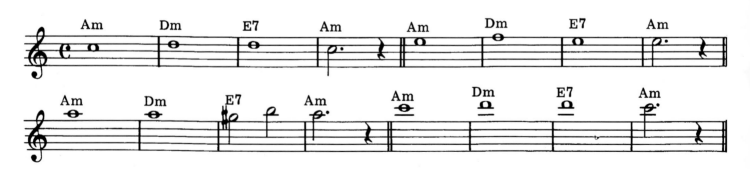

The Harmonized A Minor Scale

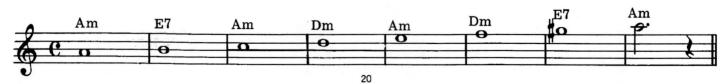

The Technical Names Of The Scale Steps

Each degree of the scale will be designated by a number and a specific technical name. Up to this point in this course we have referred only to the letter name of each degree depending on the note falling on each degree. The number of each scale degree will be in Roman numerals.

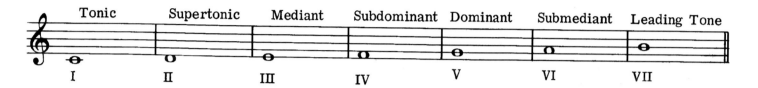

The Chromatic Scale

The Chromatic Scale is composed of *twelve Half-Steps* within an octave.

It may be written from any pitch; the Key-Signature will be that of the Major Key of the chosen pitch. It is written upward in sharps and downward in flats.

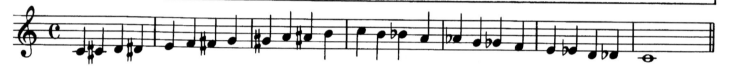

A Chord Etude In A Minor

Night Song

Mel Bay

21

Harmonizing The Non—Chordal Tones With The Am Chord

The Chordal Tones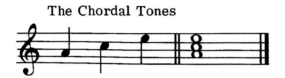

The Non-Chordal Tones

The Non-Chordal Tones Harmonized With The Am Chord

The Non-Chordal Tones Harmonized With The Dm Chord

The Chordal Tones

The Non-Chordal Tones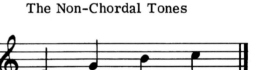

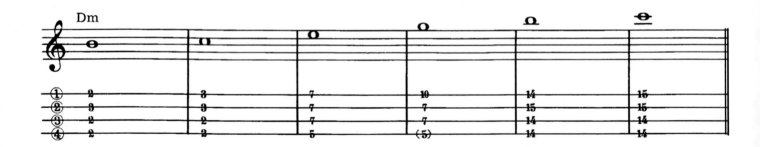

The Non-Chordal Tones Harmonized With The E7 Chord

The Chordal Tones

The Non-Chordal Tones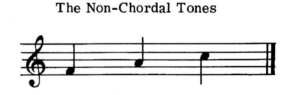

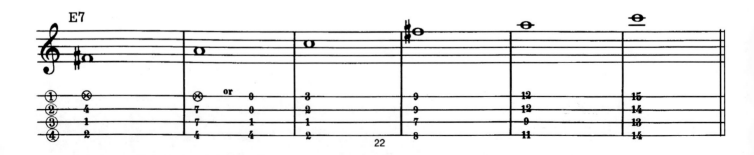

Pick—Up Notes

> One or more notes at the beginning of a strain before the first measure are referred to as pick-up notes.
>
> The rhythm for pick-up notes is taken from the last measure of the selection and the beats are counted as such. Note the three beats in the last measure of the following duet.

Danube Waves

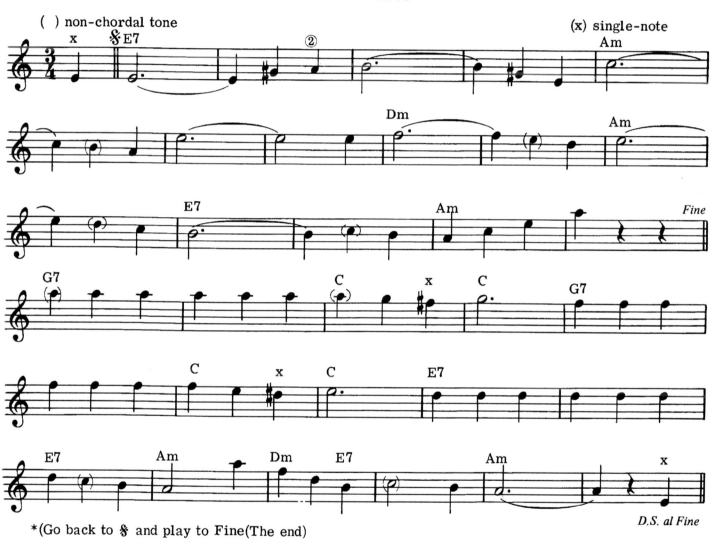

*(Go back to 𝄋 and play to Fine(The end)

D.S. al Fine

Tempo

> Tempo is the rate of speed of a musical composition.
> Three types of tempo used in this book will be:
> ANDANTE: A slow easy pace. MODERATO: Moderate. ALLEGRO: Lively.

The Key Of G

The key of G will have one sharp. (F#)
It will be identified by this signature:

The Chords In The Key Of G

The Chords in The Key of G Are: G, C & D7.

Chord Study In The Key Of G—Major

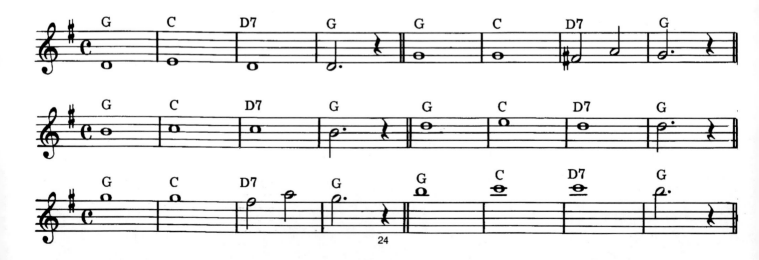

Intervals

An INTERVAL is the distance between two tones or the difference in pitch between two tones when sounded.

Intervals are measured *upward* from the lower tone to the higher.

Intervals have NUMBER names and TYPE names. For example a 3rd could be major or minor depending upon the distance.

The staff degree occupied by the lower note and the staff degree occupied by the higher note are *both included* when determining the number name of the interval.

Below are nine intervals from C to each note in the C Scale.

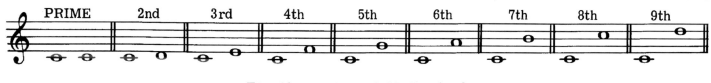

The Harmonized G Major Scale

A Chord Study In G Major
Etude

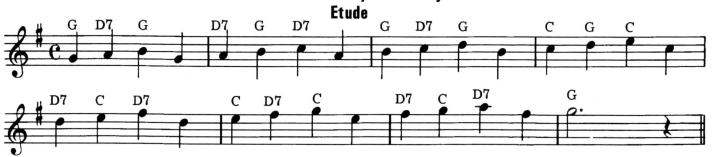

The Eighth Note

An eighth note receives one-half beat. (One quarter note equals two eighth notes).

An eighth note will have a head, stem, and flag. If two or more are in successive order they may be connected by a bar. (See Example).

Eighth Note And Eighth Rests

Skip To My Lou

⊓ = Down Stroke
V = Up-Stroke

Harmonizing The Non—Chordal Tones With The G Chord

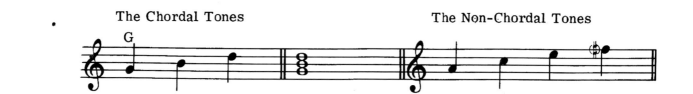

See page 16 for harmonizing the non-chordal tones with the C chord.

One exception will be the F# note.
This note will harmonize in this manner:

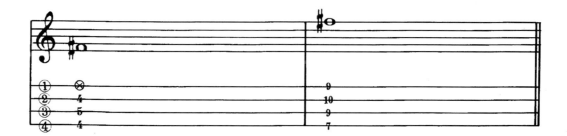

Harmonizing The Non—Chordal Tones With The D7 Chord

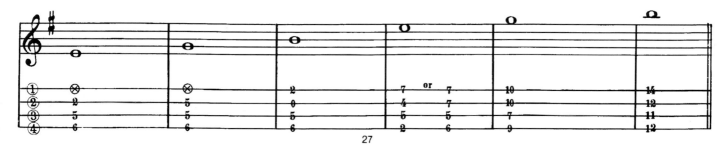

Dotted Quarter Notes

A DOT AFTER A NOTE increased its Value by ONE-HALF.

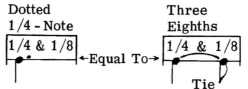

The count for the dotted quarter-note is as follows:

First And Second Endings

Sometimes two endings are required in certain selections...one to lead back into a repeated chorus and one to close it.

They will be shown like this:

The first time play the bracketed ending 1. Repeat the chorus.
The second time skip the first ending and play ending No. 2.

A Study With Non-harmonic Tones [Non-harmonic Tones ( )]

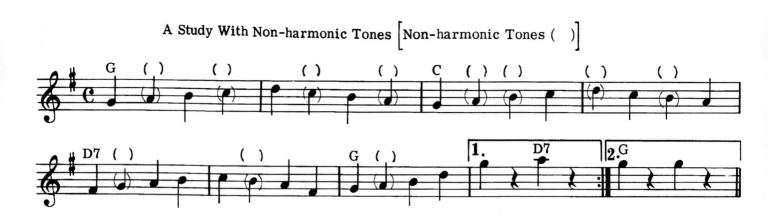

The three principal chords in each major or minor key are the tonic, sub-dominant and the dominant seventh. They are so named because they are built on the scale tones so named.

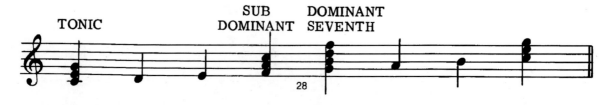

The Chords In The Key Of E Minor

Relative to G-Major

The Chords in The Key of E Minor Are: Em, Am & B7

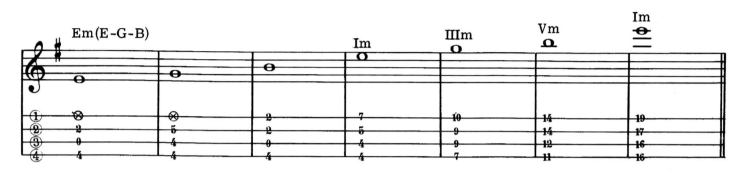

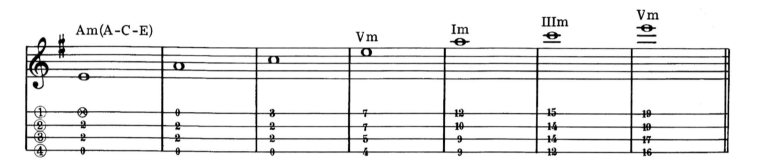

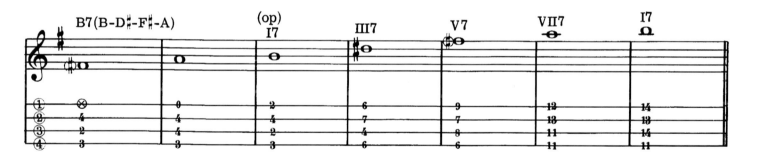

Chord Etude

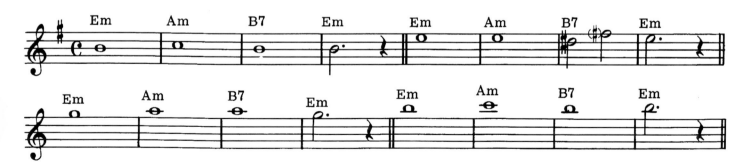

The Harmonized Scale

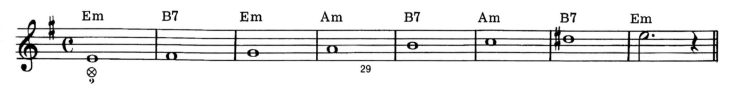

The Wayfarin' Stranger

Review....

The Technical Names Of The Scale Steps

Each degree of the scale will be designated by a number and a specific technical name. Up to this point in this course we have referred only to the letter name of each degree depending on the note falling on each degree. The number of each scale degree will be in Roman numerals.

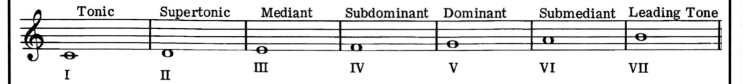

The Chromatic Scale

The Chromatic Scale is composed of *twelve Half-Steps* within an octave.

It may be written from any pitch, the Key-Signature will be that of the Major Key of the chosen pitch. It is written upward in sharps and downward in flats.

Harmonizing The Non—Chordal Tones With The Em Chord

See page 22 for the Non-Chordal tones harmonized with the Am chord.

Harmonizing The Non—Chordal Tones With The B7 Chord

Non—Chordal Study In E Minor

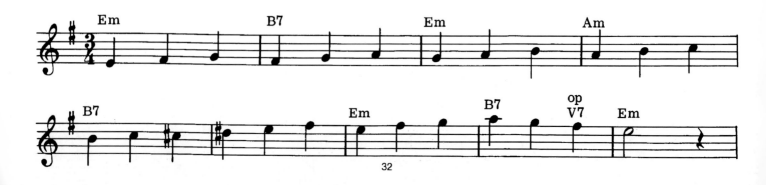

The Key Of F

The Key of F will have one flat
All B-Notes will be played one Half-Step lower as shown:

The Chords In The Key Of F

The Chords in The Key of F Are: F, B♭ & C7.

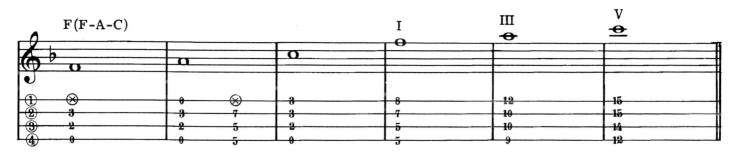

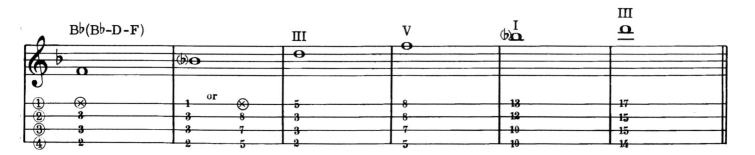

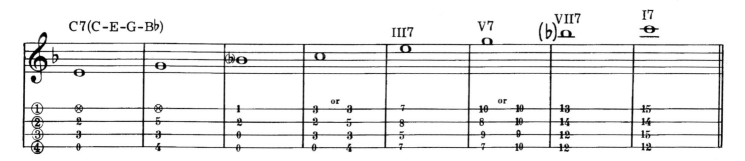

Chord Study

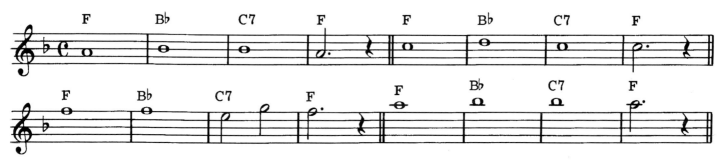

The Harmonized Scale

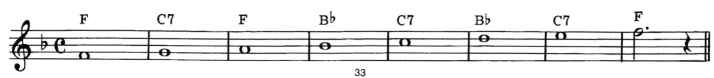

Chord Etude

Careless Love

Aunt Rhody

Harmonizing The Non—Chordal Tones With The F Chord

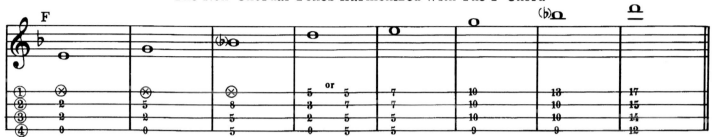

Harmonizing The Non—Chordal Tones With The B♭ Chord

Harmonizing The Non—Chordal Tones With The C7 Chord

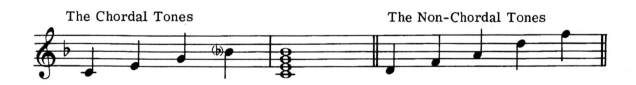
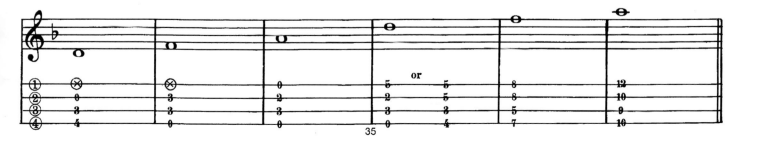

Aura Lee

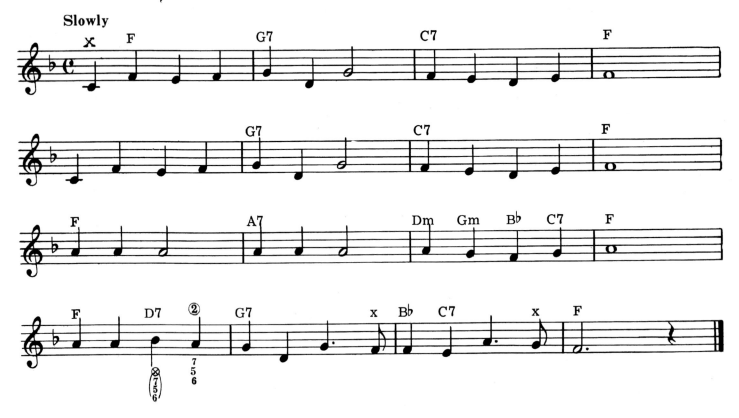

Hello My Baby

* The quarter-note triplet
  Count: 1 Tri-Plet-3-4
  Play the triplet within two beats of the measure.

The Chords In The Key Of D Minor

The Chords in The Key of D Minor Are: Dm, Gm & A7.

Relative to F major

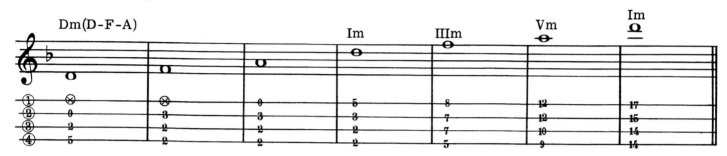

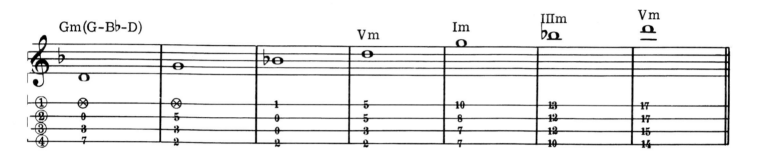

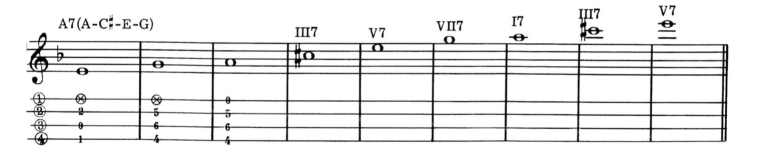

Chord Study

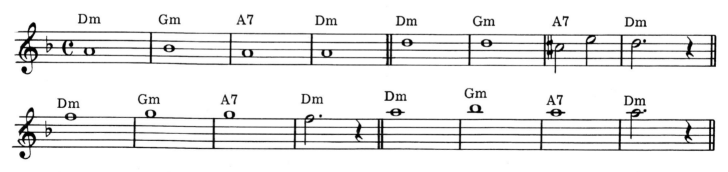

The Harmonized Scale

37

Harmonizing The Non—Chordal Tones With The Dm Chord

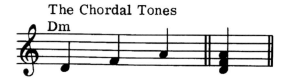

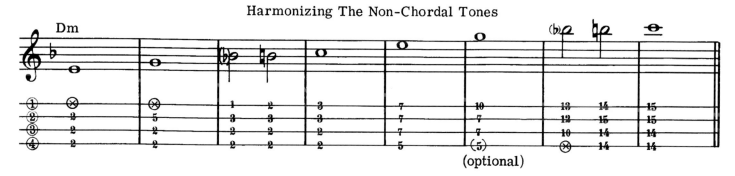

Harmonizing The Non—Chordal Tones With The Gm Chord

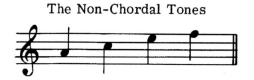
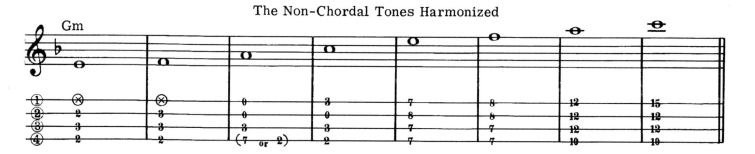

Harmonizing The Non—Chordal Tones With The A7 Chord

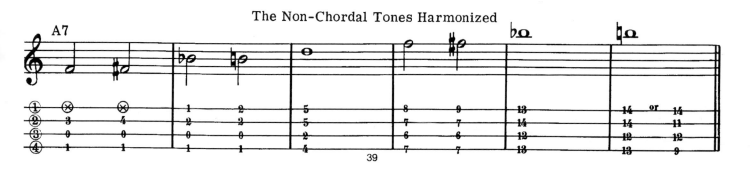

The Diminished Chords

This chord is different from all other chords in that any note of the chord may be the root. Although it is one of the most important chords in music it belongs to no key relationship. There are three principal groups of diminished chords.

The Diminished Form

Symbol for diminished is: dim. or __ . Sometimes you will see this (o) small zero used. Most modern arrangers employ the minus (−) sign.

The inversion of the chord is made by using the same formation advanced three frets higher.

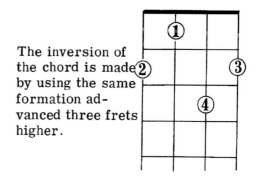

Diminished Set Number One

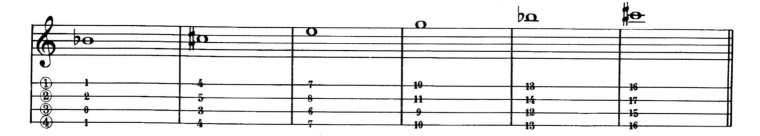

Diminished Set Number Two

Diminished Set Number Three

Bill Bailey, Wont You Please Come Home?

◠ = Pause and Hold
* Not introduced before.

The Augmented Chord

SYMBOL: Aug or (+)   The plus sign is the most commonly used symbol.

Theoretically speaking, augmented chords are produced by raising the fifth tone of the major chord one-half step.

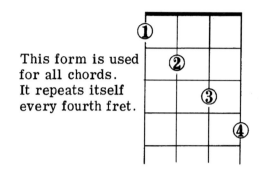

This form is used for all chords. It repeats itself every fourth fret.

Group I

Group II

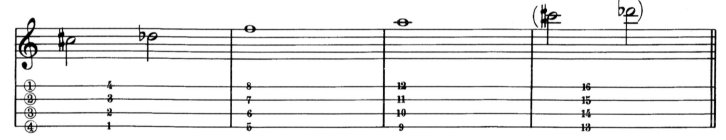

Group III

Group IV

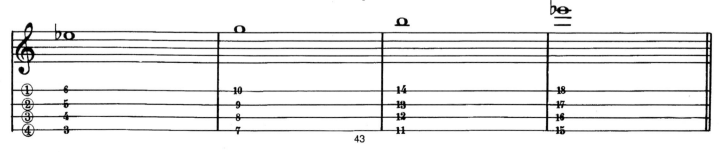

Augmented Chord Etude
(Use Augmented Form Through Out)

$\begin{pmatrix} + = \text{Aug} \\ - = \text{Dim} \end{pmatrix}$

Diminished And Augmented Etude

The Inside Augmented Chord

The Inside Diminished Chord

The Key Of B—Flat

The key of B-FLAT will have two flats. All B and E notes will be lowered 1/2 step.

The Chords In The Key Of B—Flat

The Chords in The Key of B-Flat Are: B♭, E♭ & F7

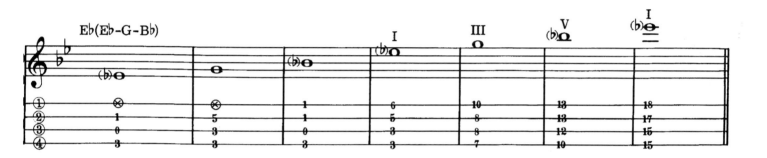

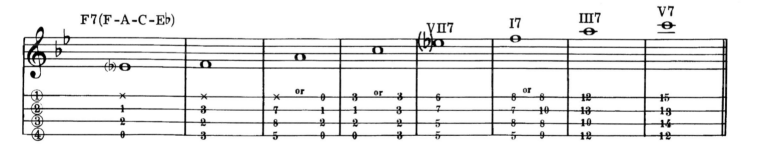

Chord Study

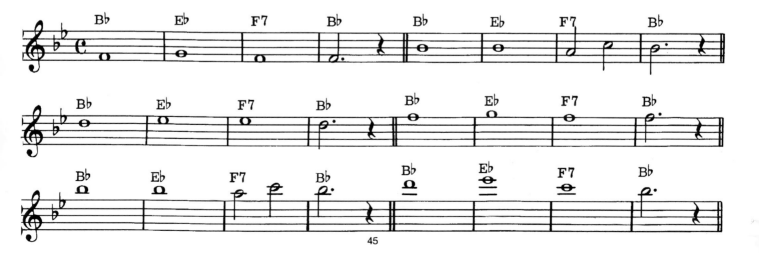

The Harmonized B♭–Major Scale

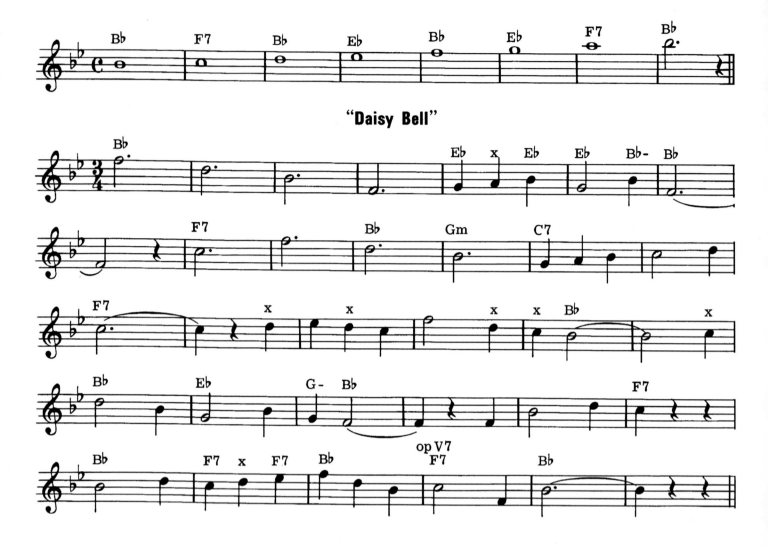

Alla—Breve Time

When Common time is to be played in a tempo too fast to conveniently count four beats, it is then best to count only two beats to each measure.

Each half measure will receive one beat.

This is referred to as "cut" time.

The time signature for Alla-Breve time will be a Vertical line drawn through the letter C as shown:

The Quarter—Note Triplet

This group of notes (♩♩♩) is used extensively in modern music.

Three quarter-notes will be played in the same time required by two.

In playing this type of triplet employ the Alla-Breve type of count.

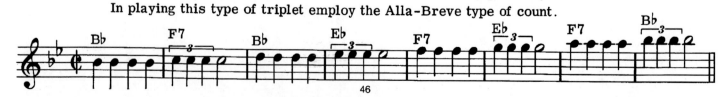

Harmonizing The Non-Chordal Tones With The B♭ Chord

The Chordal Tones   The Non-Chordal Tones

The Non-Chordal Tones Harmonized With The B♭ Chords

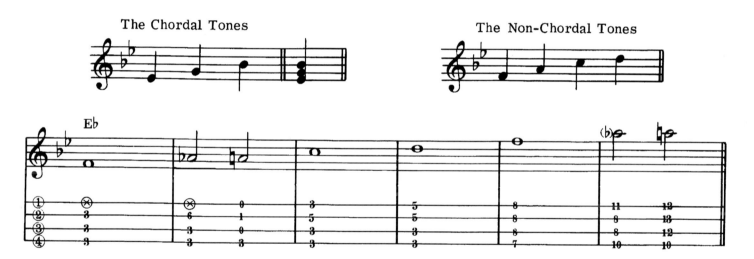

Harmonizing The Non Chordal Tones With The E♭ Chord

The Chordal Tones   The Non-Chordal Tones

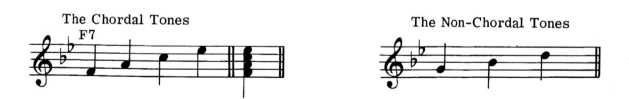

Harmonizing The Non-Chordal Tones With The F7 Chord

The Chordal Tones   The Non-Chordal Tones

The Non-Chordal Tones Harmonized With The F7 Chord

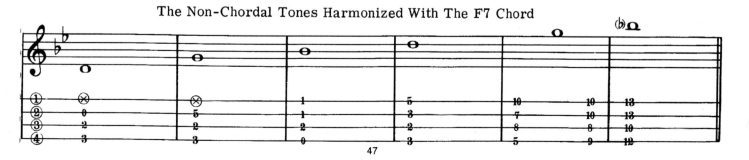

Three—Eight Time

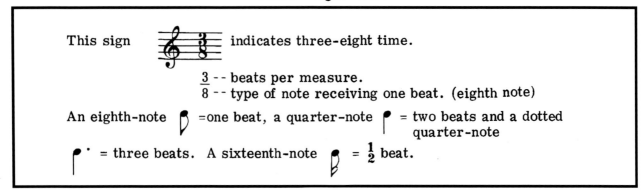

Chord Etude

Give My Regards To Broadway

G. M. Cohan

The Chords In The Key Of G Minor

The Chords in The Key of G Minor Are: Gm, Cm & D7

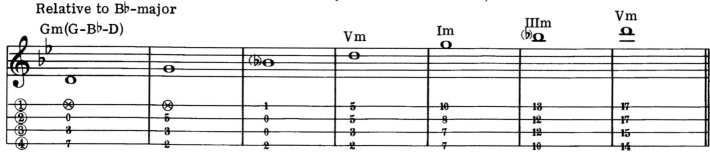

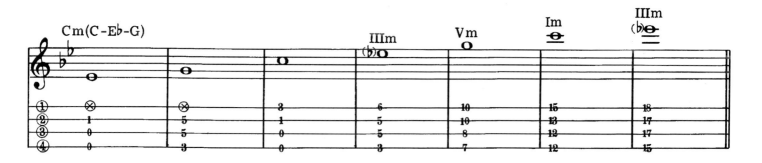

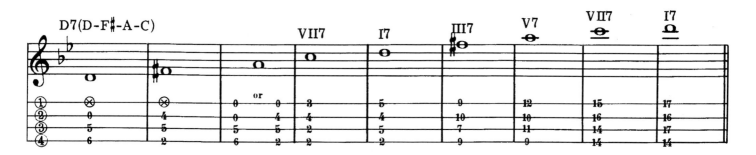

Chord Etude

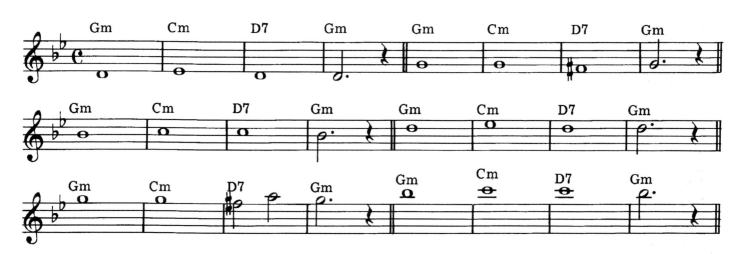

The Harmonized G Minor Scale

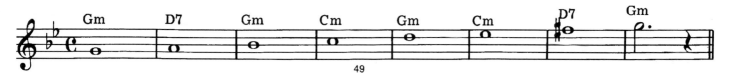

The Key Of D Major

The Key of D Major will have two sharps—F♯ and C♯.

The Chords In The Key Of D

The Chords in The Key of D Are: D, G, & A7

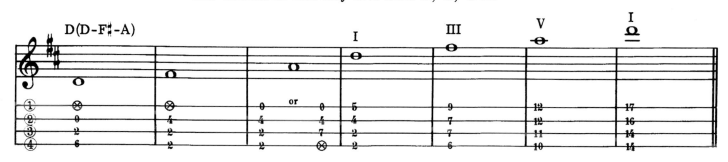

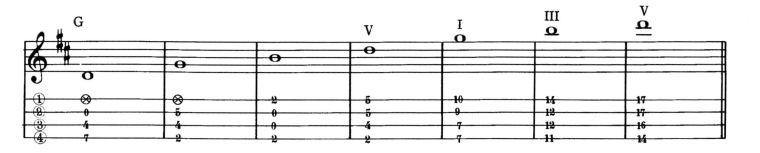

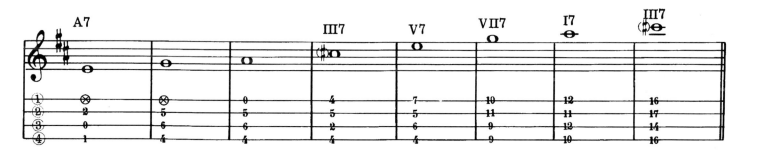

Chord Etude

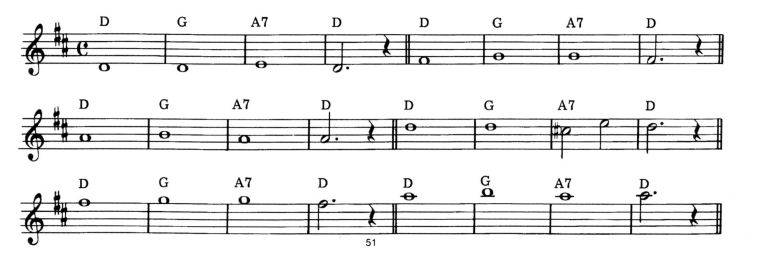

The Harmonized D Major Scale

Around Her Hair She Wore A Yellow Ribbon

Table Of Notes And Rests

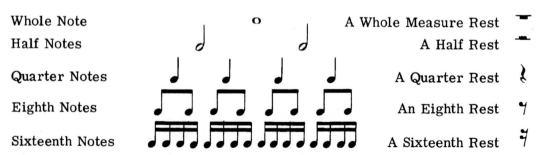

Harmonizing The Non—Chordal Tones With The D Chord

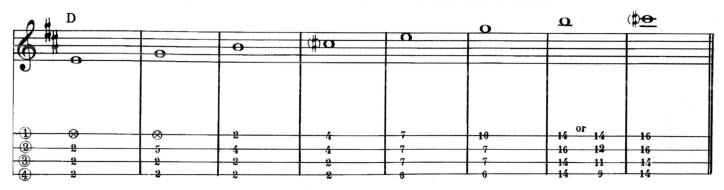

See page 27 for harmonizing non-chordal tones with the G chord.
See page 39 for harmonizing non-chordal chords with the A7 chord.

A Non Chordal Study In D

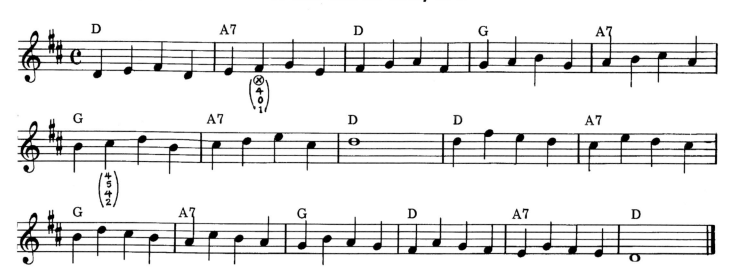

More Chromatic Signs

Up to this point we have studied and used the Sharp (♯), the Flat (♭), and the Natural (♮). The student is familiar by now with their function. We now introduce the Double-Sharp and the Double-Flat.

𝄪 = Double-Sharp. A Double-Sharp will raise the sound of a tone two frets.
♭♭ = Double Flat. A Double-Flat will lower the sound of a tone two frets.

A natural will cancel all sharps, flats, double-sharps and double-flats. If a note has been double-sharped or double flatted, the return to one sharp or flat will require a natural sign followed by the desired sharp or flat.

The Key Of B Minor

(Relative to D Major)

The Chords in The Key of B Minor Are: Bm, Em & F#7.

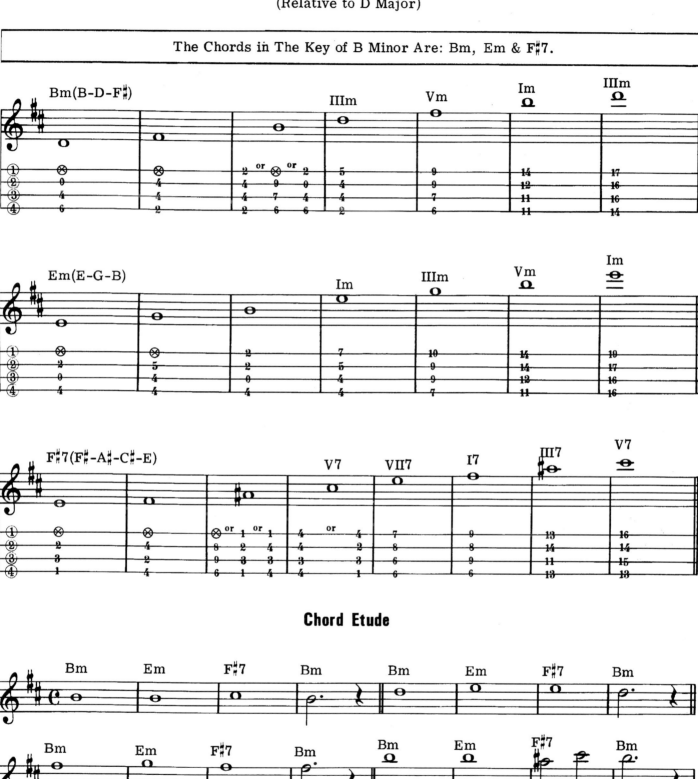

Chord Etude

The Harmonized Scale

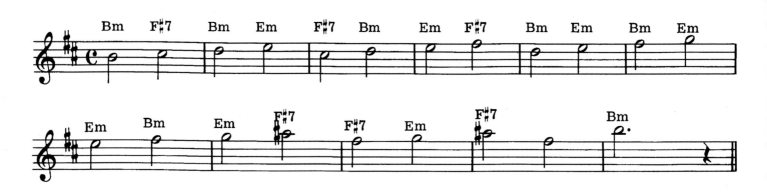

Harmonizing The Non Chordal Tones With The Bm Chord

The Chordal Tones

The Non-Chordal Tones

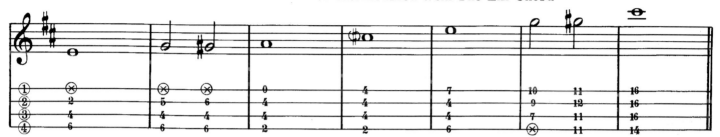
The Non-Chordal Tones Harmonized With The Em Chord

Harmonizing The Non—Chordal Tones With The Em Chord

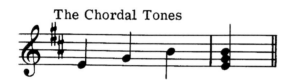
The Chordal Tones

The Non-Chordal Tones

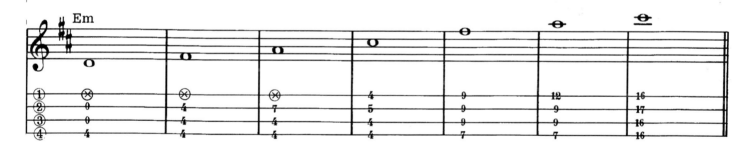

Harmonizing The Non—Chordal Tones With The F#7 Chord

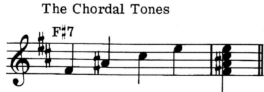
The Chordal Tones

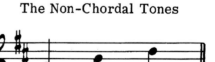
The Non-Chordal Tones

The Non-Chordal Tones Harmonized With The F#7 Chord

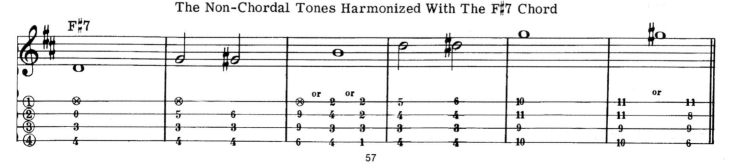

The Key Of E Flat Major

The B; E and A notes will be played 1/2 step lower.

The Chords In The Key Of E Flat

The Chords in The Key of E-Flat Are: E♭, A♭ & B♭7.

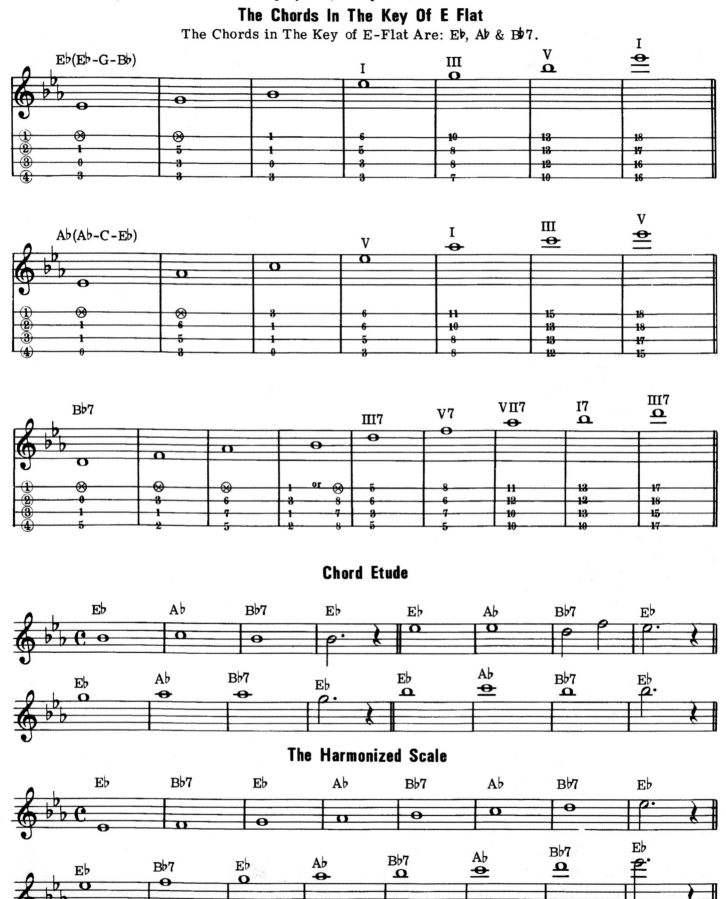

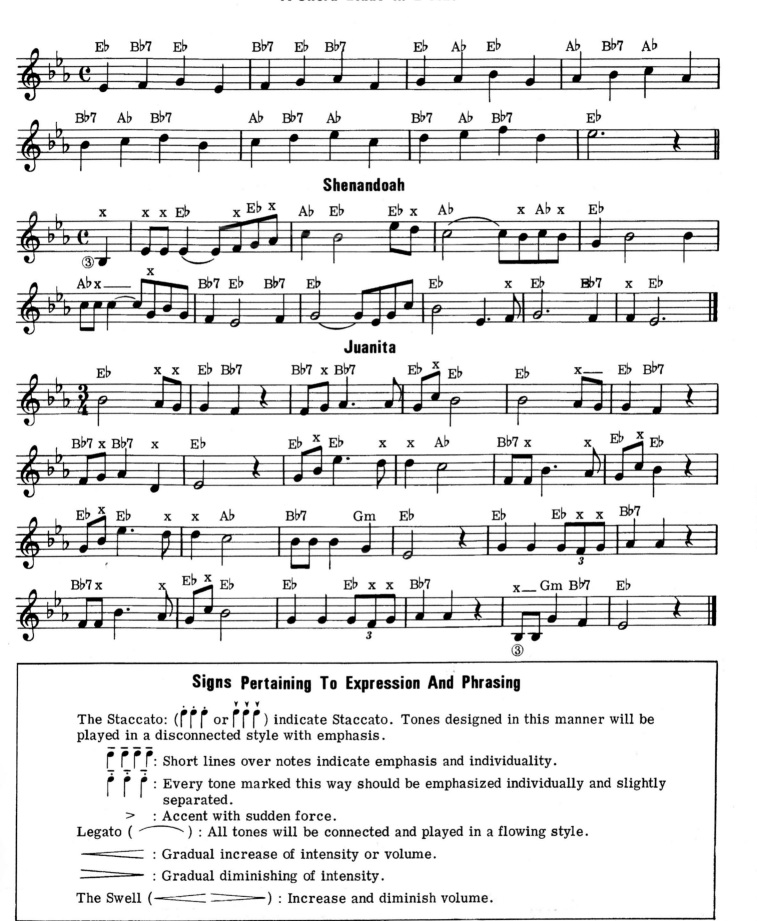

The Non Chordal Tones Harmonized With The E♭ Chords

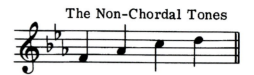
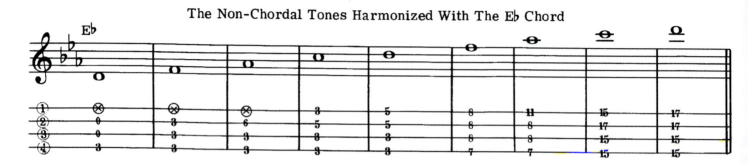

Harmonizing The Non—Chordal Tones With The A♭ Chord

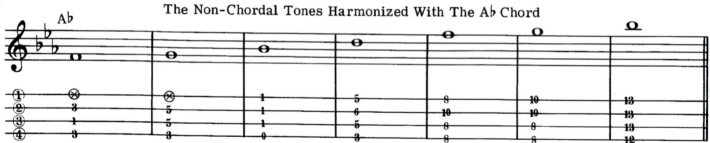

The Non Chordal Tones Harmonized With The B♭7 Chord

The Chords In The Key Of C Minor
(Relative to E♭ Major)

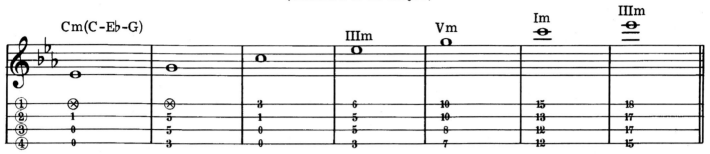

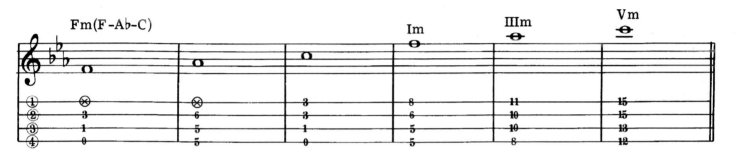

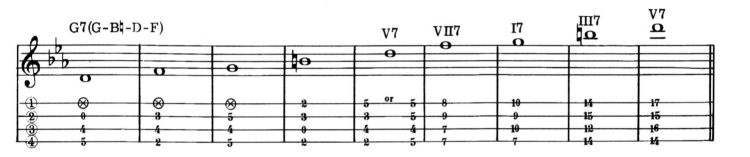

Chord Study

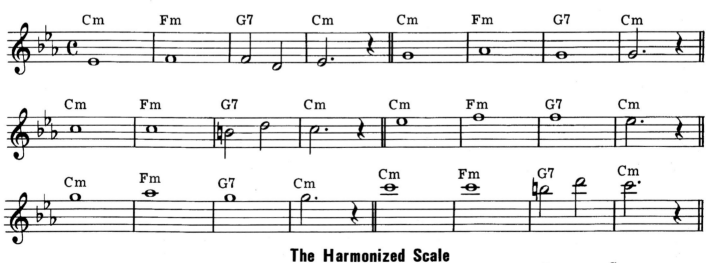

The Harmonized Scale

Harmonizing The Non-Chordal Tones With The Cm Chord

The Chordal Tones 　　The Non-Chordal Tones

The Non-Chordal Tones Harmonized With The Cm Chord

Harmonizing The Non-Chordal Tones With The Fm Chord

The Chordal Tones 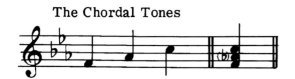　　The Non-Chordal Tones

The Non-Chordal Tones Harmonized With The Fm Chord

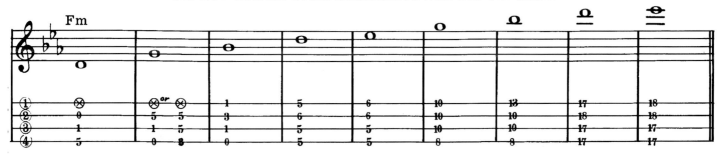

See page 16 for the non-chordal tones with the G7 chord.
The following will be the A♭ and E♭ tones harmonized.

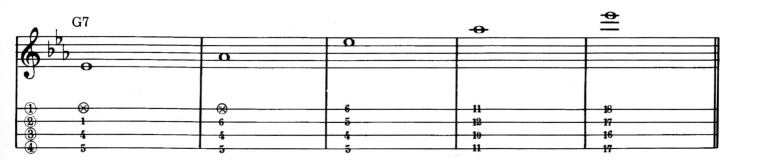

The Chords In The Key Of A Major

The Chords in The Key of A Are: A, D & E7.

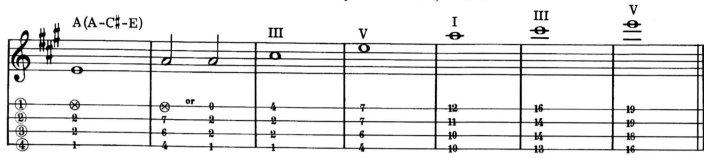

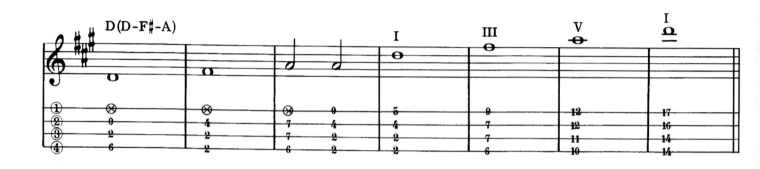

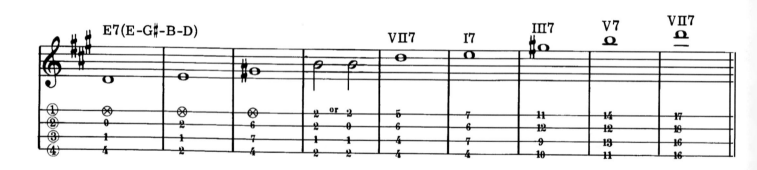

A Chord Study In A Major

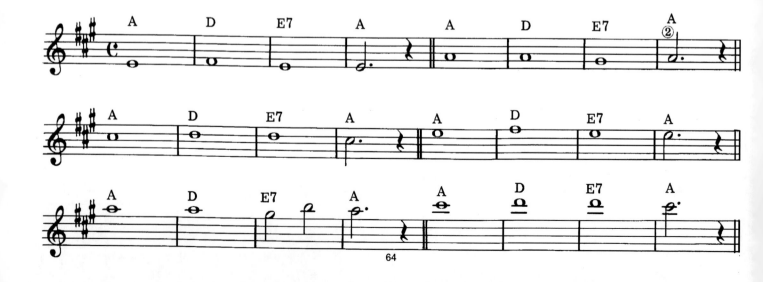

The Harmonized A Major Scale

Chord Etude

In The Evening By The Moonlight

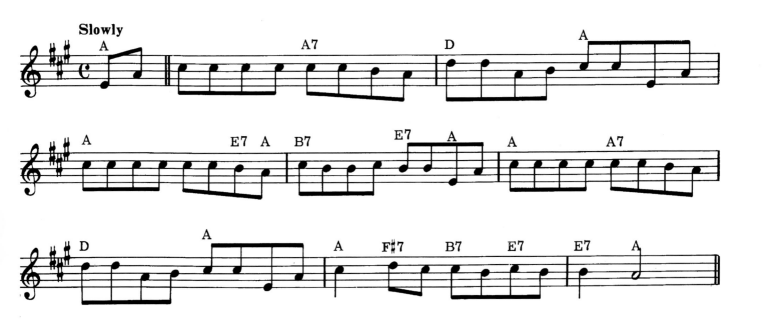

The Non Chordal Tones Harmonizing With The A, D, And E7 Chords

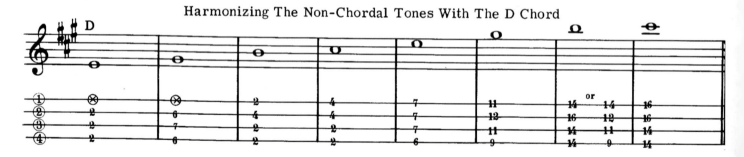

The Non—Chordal Tones Harmonizing With The D Chord

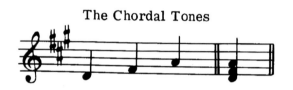

The Non Chordal Tones Harmonizing With The E7 Chord

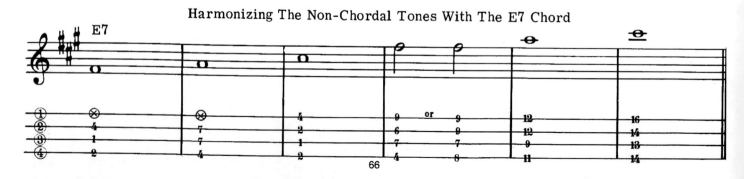

The Band Played On

Melody

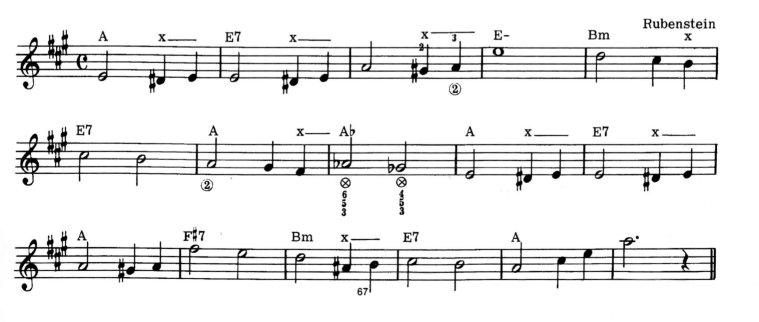

Rubenstein

The Chords In The Key Of F# Minor

(Relative to A Major)

The Chords in The Key of F# Minor Are: F#m, Bm & C#7

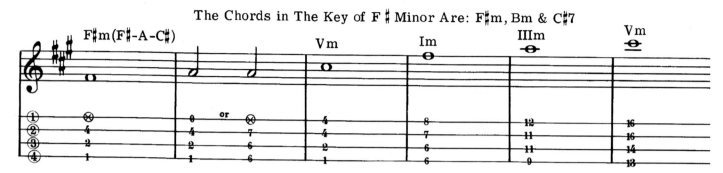

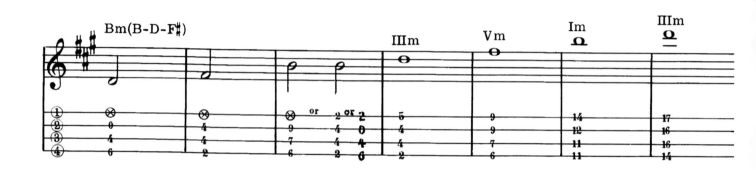

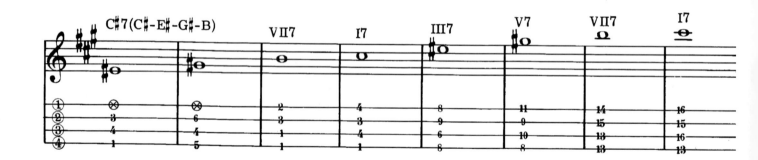

Chord Study

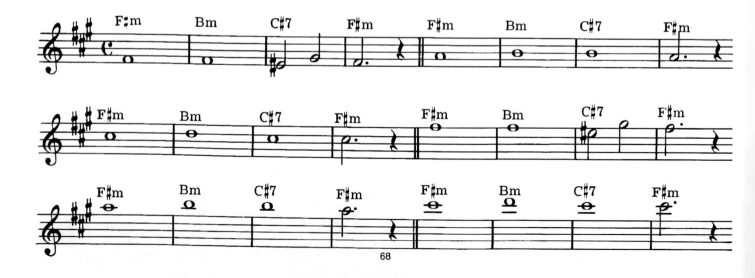

The Non Chordal Tones Harmonized With The F Sharp Minor Chord

The Chordal Tones

The Non-Chordal Tones

Harmonizing The Non-Chordal Tones With F#m

Harmonizing The Non—Chordal Tones With The Bm Chord

The Chordal Tones

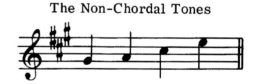
The Non-Chordal Tones

The Non-Chordal Tones Harmonized With Bm

The Non Chordal Tones Harmonized With The C#7 Chord

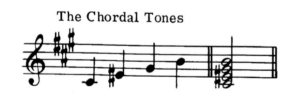
The Chordal Tones

The Non-Chordal Tones

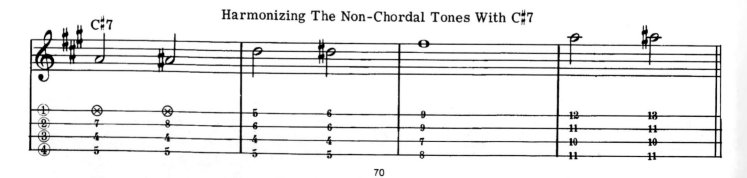
Harmonizing The Non-Chordal Tones With C#7

The Key Of A Flat

The key of A-FLAT will have FOUR FLATS. All B, E, A and D will be lowed 1/2 step. The flatted notes are easy to remember by spelling b-e-a-d.

The Chords In The Key Of A Flat

The Chords in The Key of A-Flat Are: Ab, Db and Eb7

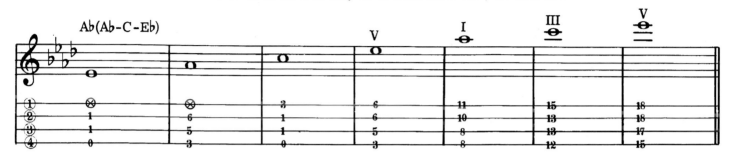

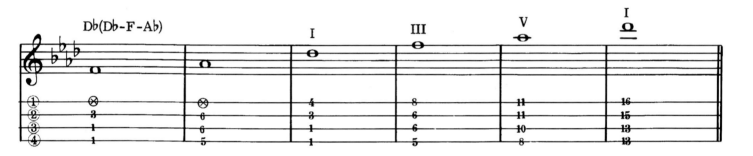

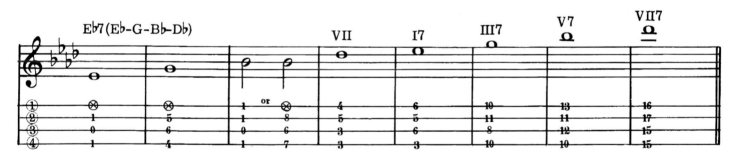

Chord Etude

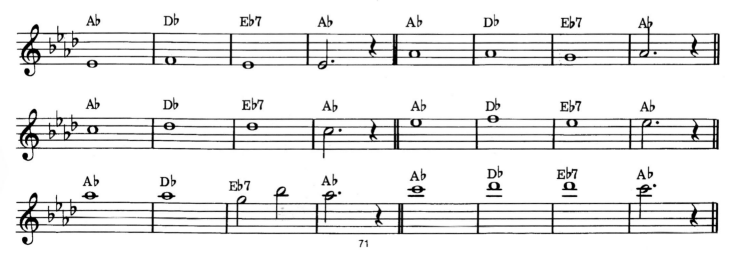

The Harmonized A Flat Major Scale

The Chord Etude In A Flat

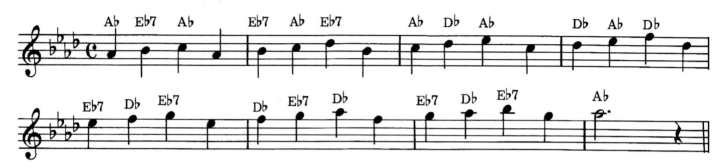

"You Tell Me Your Dream"

How Can I Leave Thee

Harmonizing The Non-Chordal Tones With The A♭ Chord

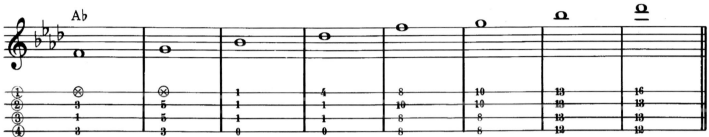

Harmonizing The Non-Chordal Tones With The D♭ Chord

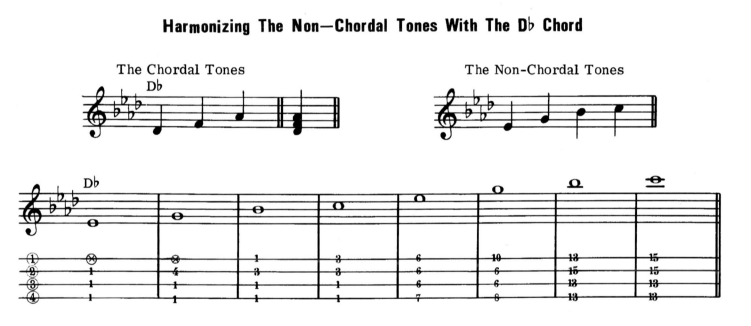

Harmonizing The Non-Chordal Tones With The E♭7 Chord

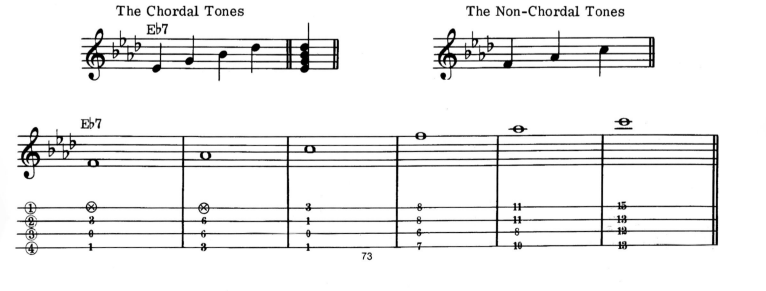

The Chords In The Key Of F Minor
(Relative to The Key of A Flat)

The Chords in The Key of F Minor Are: Fm, Bbm & C7

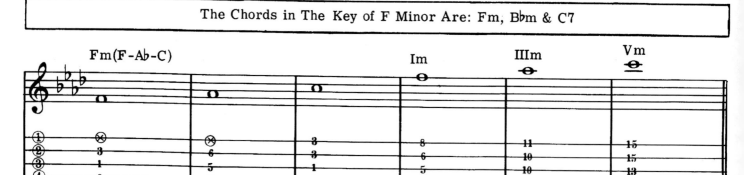

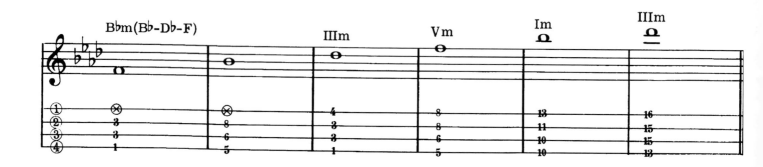

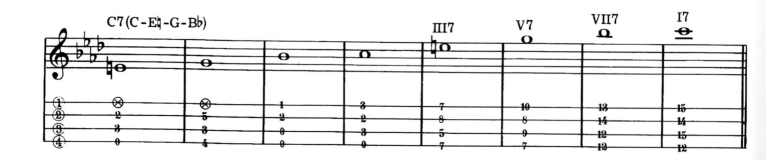

Chord Etude

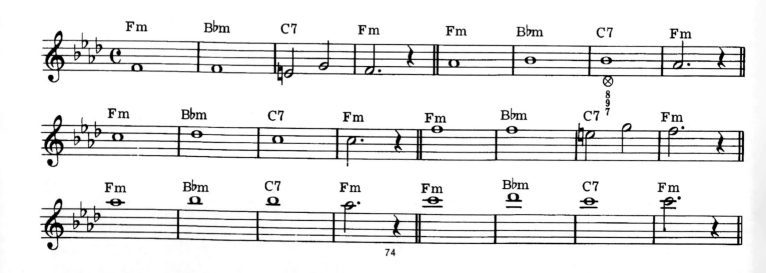

The Harmonized F Minor Scale

Chord Etude In F Minor

Minka

See page 61 for harmonizing the non-chordal tones with the Fm chord.

Harmonizing The Non—Chordal Tones With The B♭m Chord

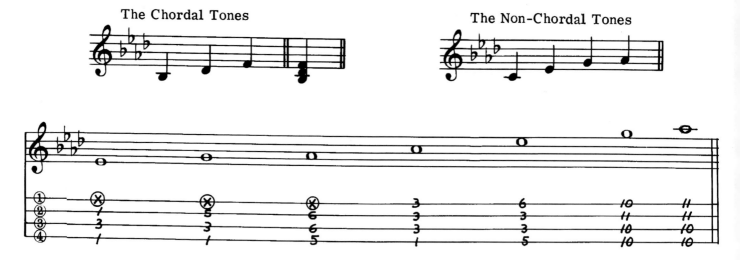

See page 35 for harmonizing the non-chordal tones with the C7 chord.
Use the diminished for harmonizing the D-Flat note.

Greensleeves

76

The Key Of E Major

The key of E will have four sharps. All F, C, G, and D notes will be sharped.

The Chords In The Key Of E Major

The Chords in The Key of E Major Are: E, A & B7.

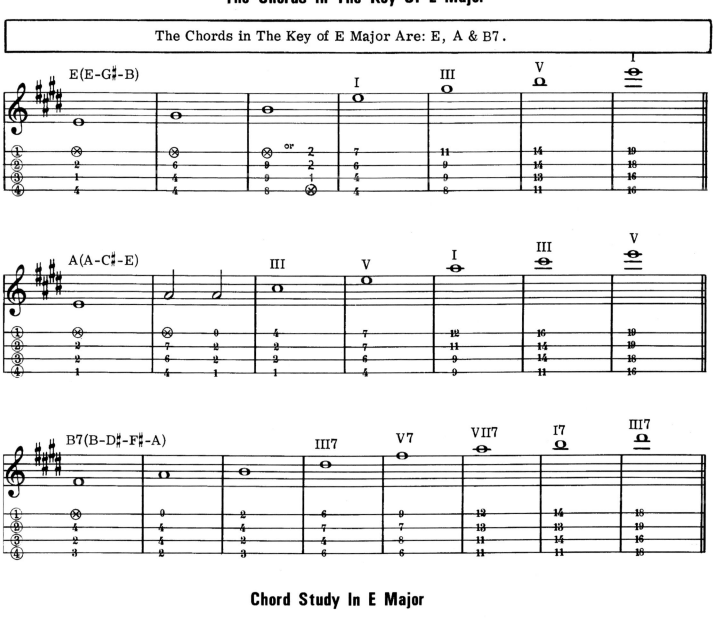

Chord Study In E Major

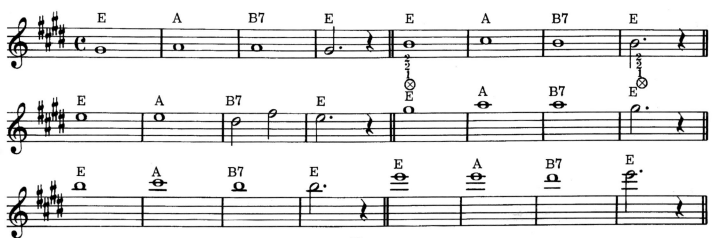

The Harmonized Scale

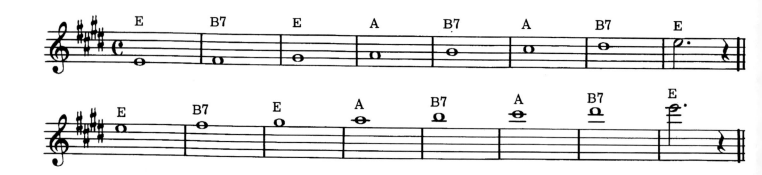

Chord Etude

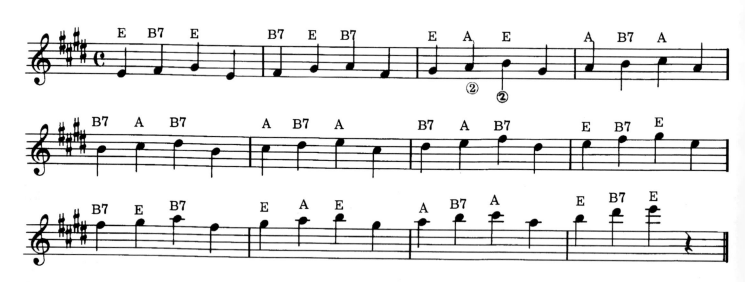

Camptown Races

Harmonizing The Non—Chordal Tones With The E Chord

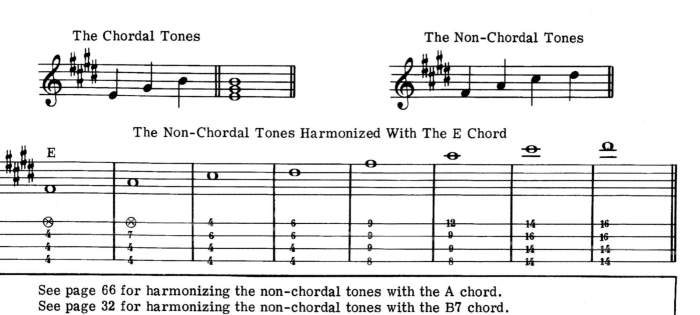

See page 66 for harmonizing the non-chordal tones with the A chord.
See page 32 for harmonizing the non-chordal tones with the B7 chord.

A Non Chordal Study

(Go back to the beginning and end at "Fine"

The Chords In The Key Of C Sharp Minor

Relative to E Major
The Chord in The Key of C-Sharp Minor Are: C#m, F#m and G#7.

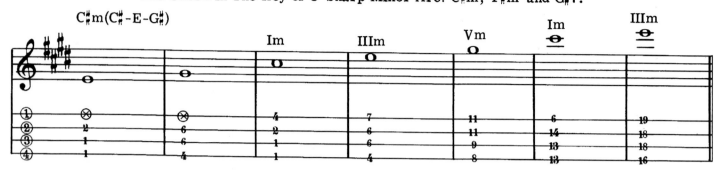

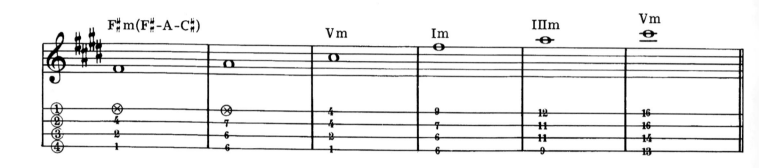

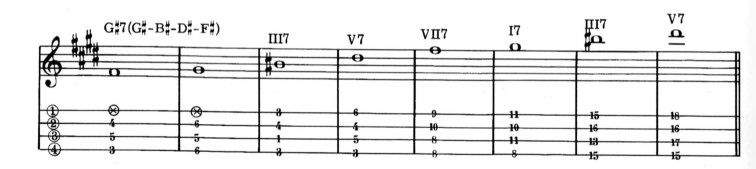

Chord Study

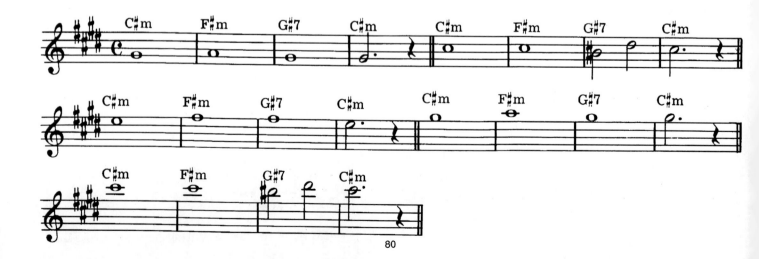

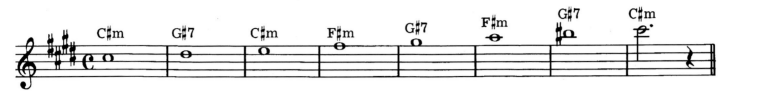
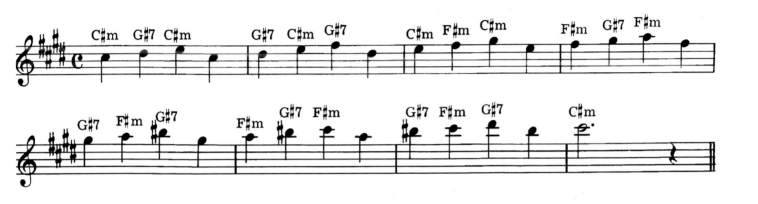

Harmonizing The Non Chordal Tones With The C#m Chord

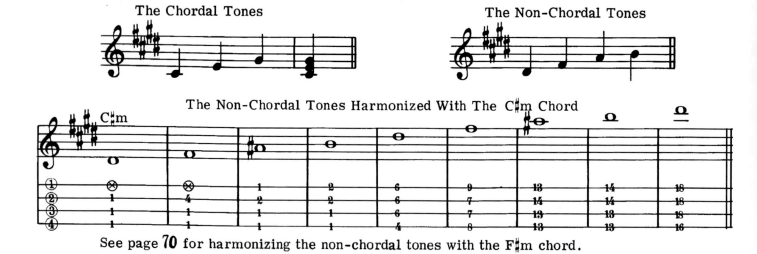

See page 70 for harmonizing the non-chordal tones with the F#m chord.

Harmonizing The Non Chordal Tones With The G#7 Chord

Gypsy Love Song

VICTOR HERBERT
Arr. Mel Bay

The Key Of D Flat Major

The B, E, A, D and G notes will be lowered 1/2 step.

The Chords In The Key Of D♭ Major

The Chords in The Key of D♭ Major Are: D♭, G♭ & A♭7

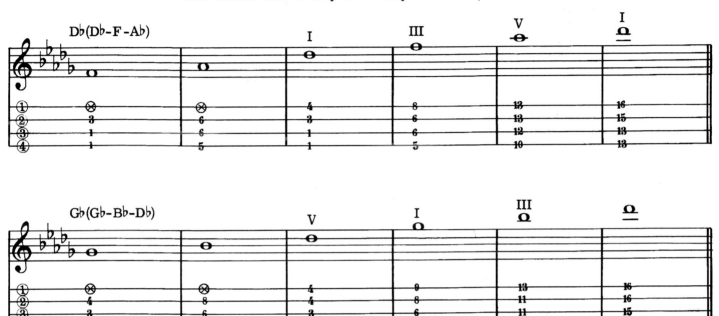

Chord Etude

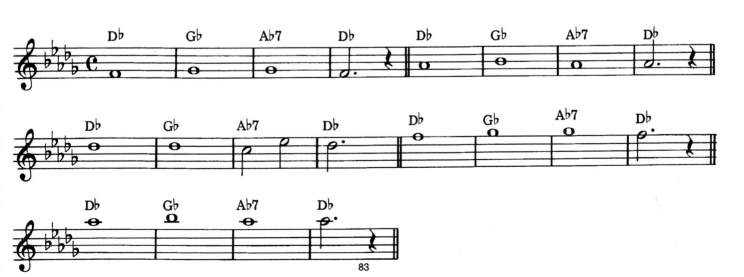

The Harmonized Scale

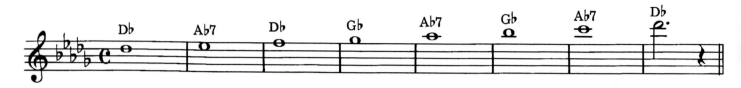

A Chord Etude

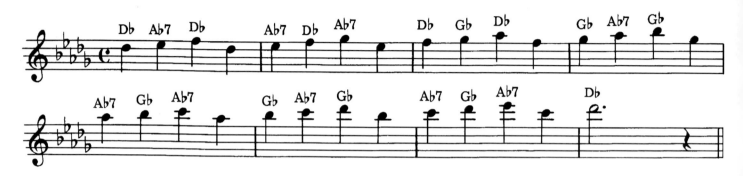

The Caisson Song

Harmonizing The Non-Chordal Tones With The D♭ Chord

The Chordal Tones

The Non-Chordal Tones

The Non-Chordal Tones Harmonized With The D♭ Chord

Harmonizing The Non-Chordal Tones With The G♭ Chord

The Chordal Tones

The Non-Chordal Tones

The Non-Chordal Tones Harmonized With The G♭ Chord
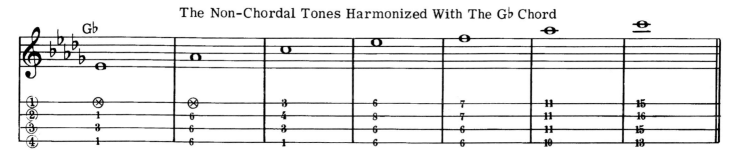

Harmonizing The Non Chordal Tones With The A♭7 Chord

The Chordal Tones

The Non-Chordal Tones

The Non-Chordal Tones Harmonized With The A♭7 Chord
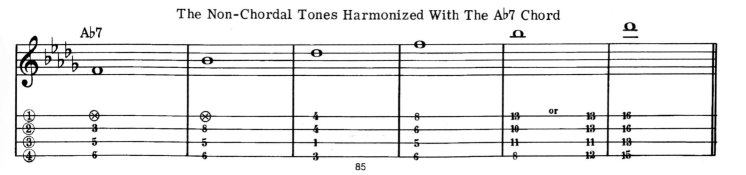

The Chords In The Key Of B Flat Minor

The Chords in The Key of B-Flat Minor Are: Bbm, Ebm & F7

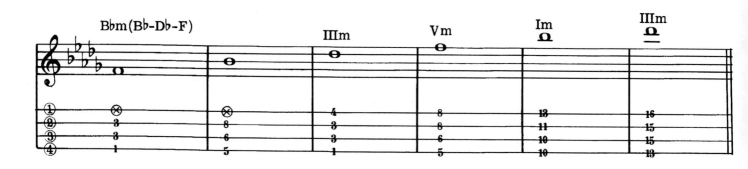

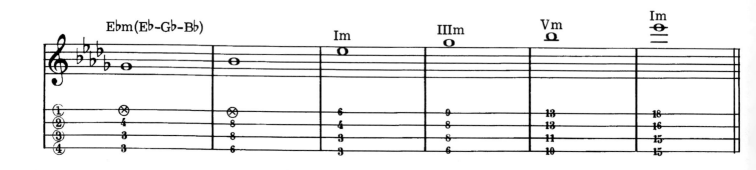

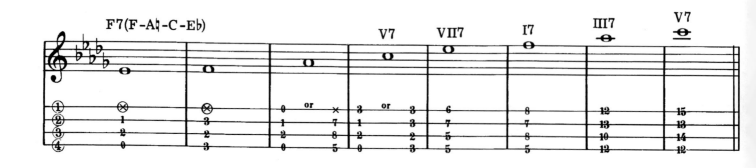

A Chord Study In B Flat Minor

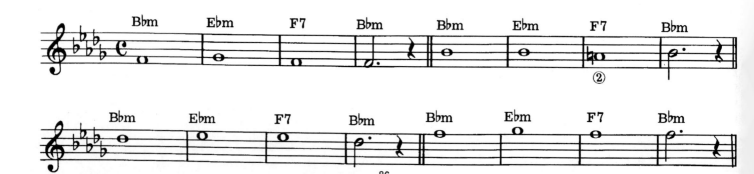

The B Flat Minor Scale Harmonized

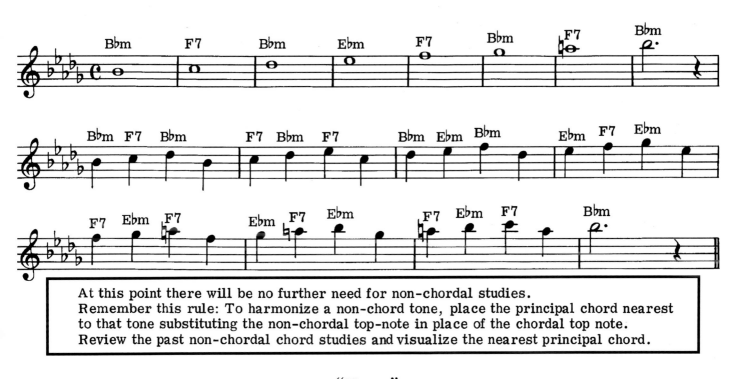

At this point there will be no further need for non-chordal studies.
Remember this rule: To harmonize a non-chord tone, place the principal chord nearest to that tone substituting the non-chordal top-note in place of the chordal top note.
Review the past non-chordal chord studies and visualize the nearest principal chord.

"Moses"

Folk Song

Tenuto (∧) : Hold the tone its full value.

Luft Pause (//) : An exaggerated pause. Usually follows a note that is held by a hold sign.
Example: (fermata)

The Comma (,) is used sometimes to indicate an interruption in the flow of tone.

The Key Of B Major

The key of B-MAJOR has five sharps. (F♯-C♯-G♯-D♯ & A♯)

The Chords In The Key of B Major

The Chords in The Key of B Major Are: B, E & F♯7

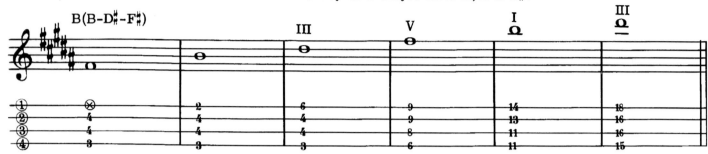

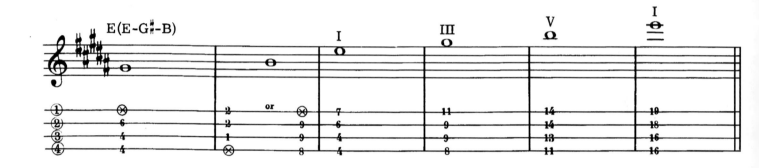

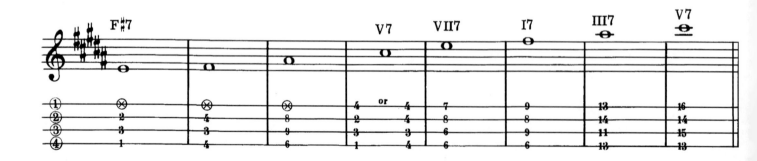

Chord Etude In B Major

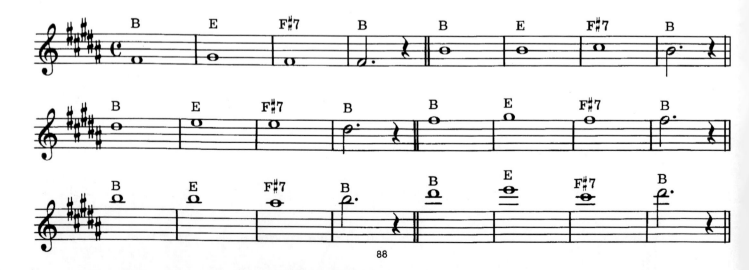

The Harmonized B Major Scale

A Chord Etude

The Yellow Rose Of Texas

The Chords In The Key Of G Sharp Minor
(Relative to B Major)

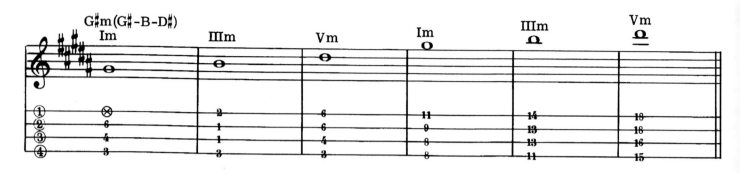
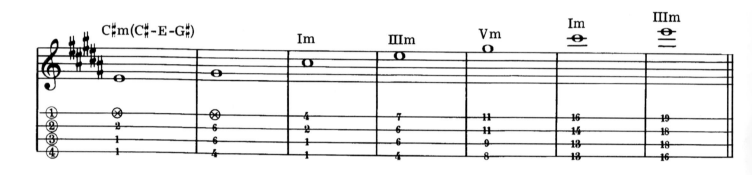
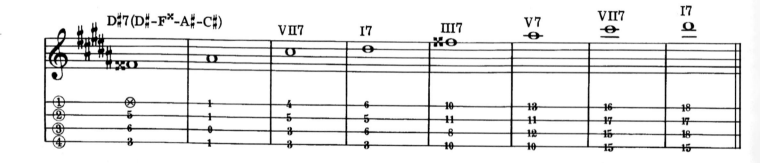

Chord Etude

The Harmonized G Sharp Minor Scale

A Chord Etude In G Sharp Minor

The Volga Boatman

Repeat at a faster tempo.

The Keys Of F Sharp And G Flat Major

The key of F-Sharp has six sharps. They are F#, C#, G# D#, A# and E#.
The key of G-Flat has six flats. They are Bb, Eb, Ab Db, Gb and Cb.
THEY ARE ENHARMONIC KEYS AND WILL BE DEVELOPED TOGETHER.

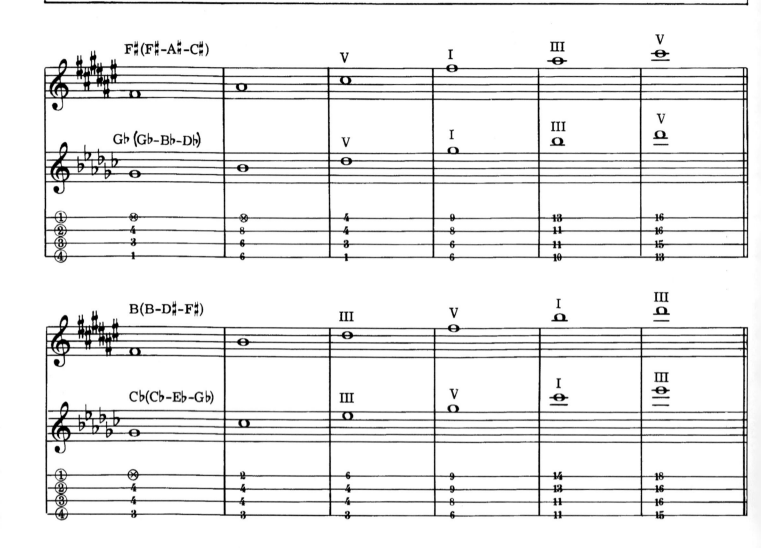

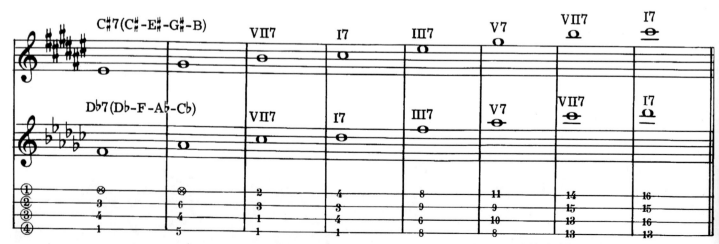

A Chord Study

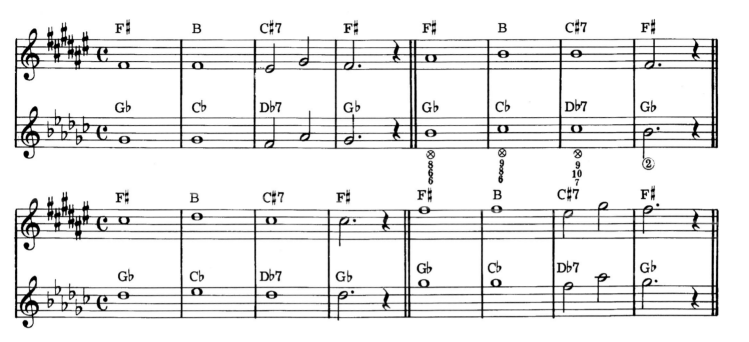

The Harmonized Scale

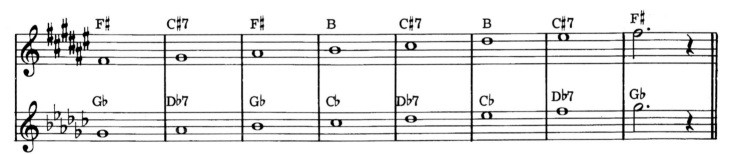

The Streets Of Laredo

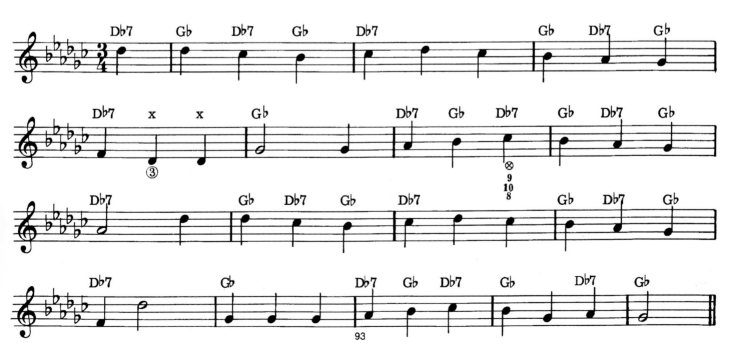

The Chords In The Keys Of D Sharp And E Flat Minor

(Relative to F-Sharp And G-Flat Major)

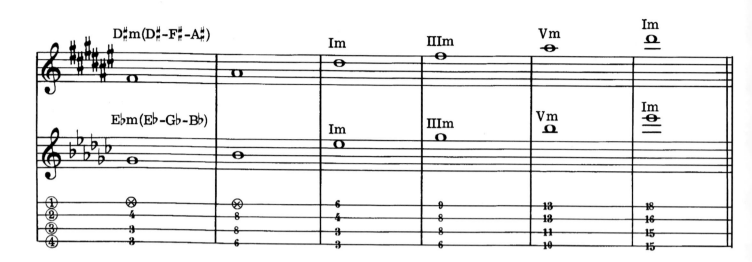

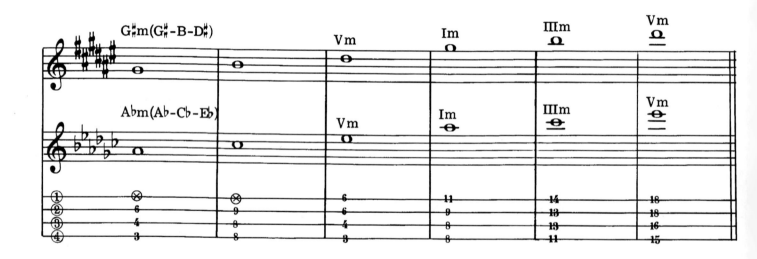

Chord Study

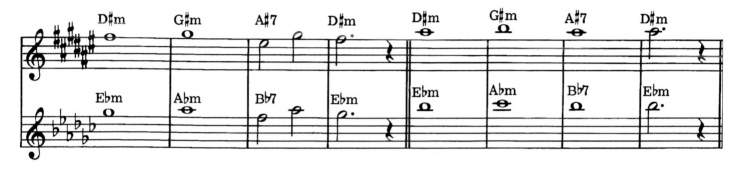

The Harmonized Scale

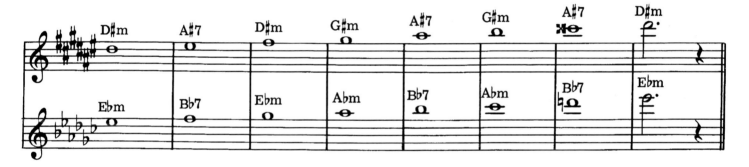

A Review Of The Chord Spelling

	MAJOR	MINOR	SEVENTH	DIMINISHED	AUGMENTED
C	C-E-G	C-Eb-G	C-E-G-Bb	C-Eb-F#-A	C-E-G#
F	F-A-C	F-Ab-C	F-A-C-Eb	F-Ab-B-D	F-A-C#
Bb	Bb-D-F	Bb-Db-F	Bb-D-F-Ab	Bb-Db-E-G	Bb-D-F#
Eb	Eb-G-Bb	Eb-Gb-Bb	Eb-G-Bb-Db	Eb-Gb-A-C	Eb-G-B
Ab	Ab-C-Eb	Ab-Cb-Eb	Ab-C-Eb-Gb	Ab-B-D-F	Ab-C-E
Db	Db-F-Ab	Db-Fb-Ab	Db-F-Ab-Cb	Db-Fb-G-Bb	Db-F-A
Gb	Gb-Bb-Db	Gb-Bbb-Db	Gb-Bb-Db-Fb	Gb-A-C-Eb	Gb-Bb-D
F#	F#-A#-C#	F#-A-C#	F#-A#-C#-E	F#-A-C-Eb	F#-A#-C×
B	B-D#-F#	B-D-F#	B-D#-F#-A	B-D-F-Ab	B-D#-F×
E	E-G#-B	E-G-B	E-G#-B-D	E-G-Bb-Db	E-G#-B#
A	A-C#-E	A-C-E	A-C#-E-G	A-C-Eb-Gb	A-C#-E#
D	D-F#-A	D-F-A	D-F#-A-C	D-F-Ab-Cb	D-F#-A#
G	G-B-D	G-Bb-D	G-B-D-A	G-Bb-Db-Fb	G-B-D#

Special Note: By changing the note spelling in the diminished chords, we avoided double sharps and double flats.

We substituted the enharmonic tones.

The Major Sixth Chords

Symbol = 6

The major sixth chord is a great substitute for the major chord.
It is made up employing the 1st, 3rd, 5th and sixth notes of the major scale.

Example

The Major-Sixth Forms

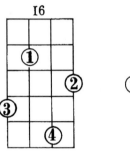
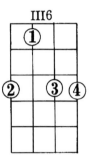
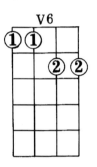
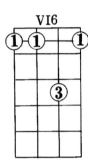
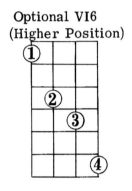

The Inversions

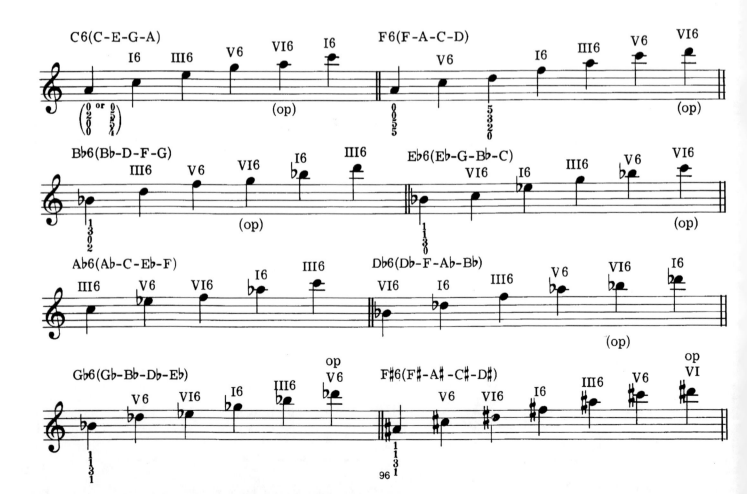

The Sixth Chord Inversions

A Sixth Chord Etude

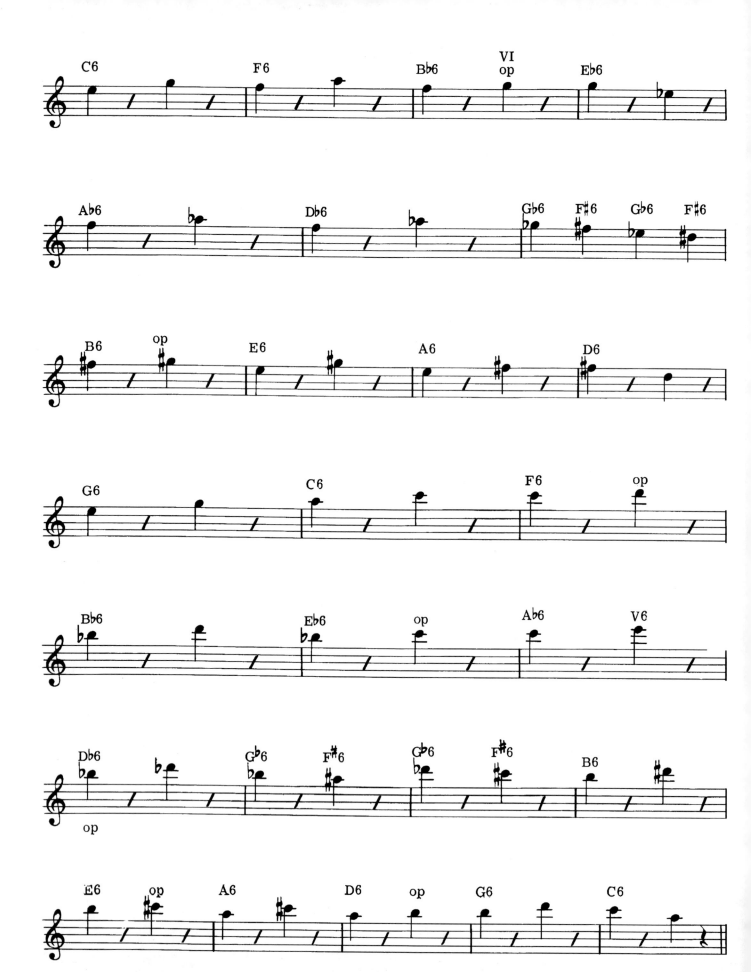

The Minor-Sixth Chords

Symbol = m6

The minor - sixth chord is made by lowering the third 1/2 step.

◇ = 3rd before lowering.

The Minor-Sixth Chord Forms

(The ◇ = The Natural Third)

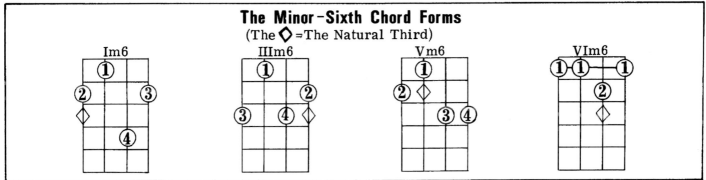

The Inversions

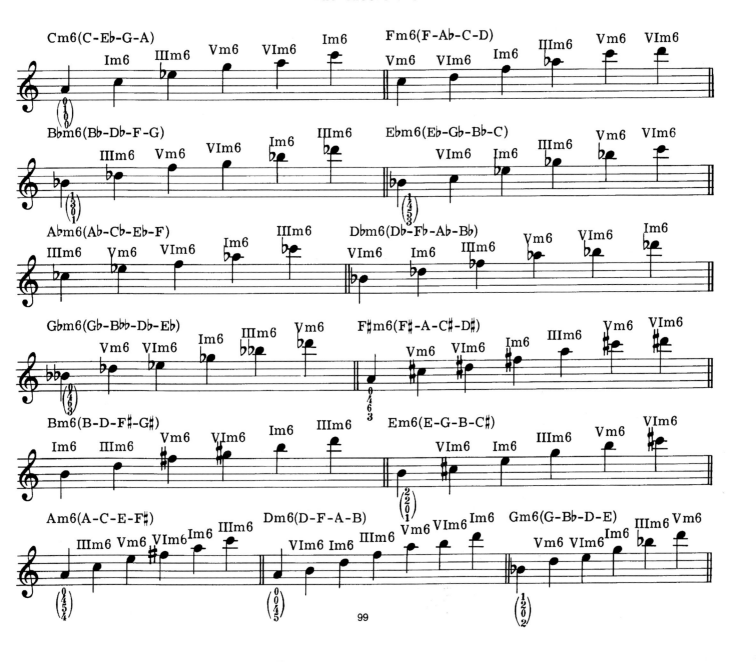

Sixth To Minor-Sixth Etude

The Major-Seventh Chords

Symbol = Ma7

The major-seventh chord consists of the 1st, 3rd, 5th and 7th notes of the major scale.

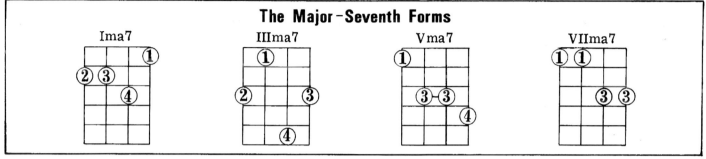

The Inversions

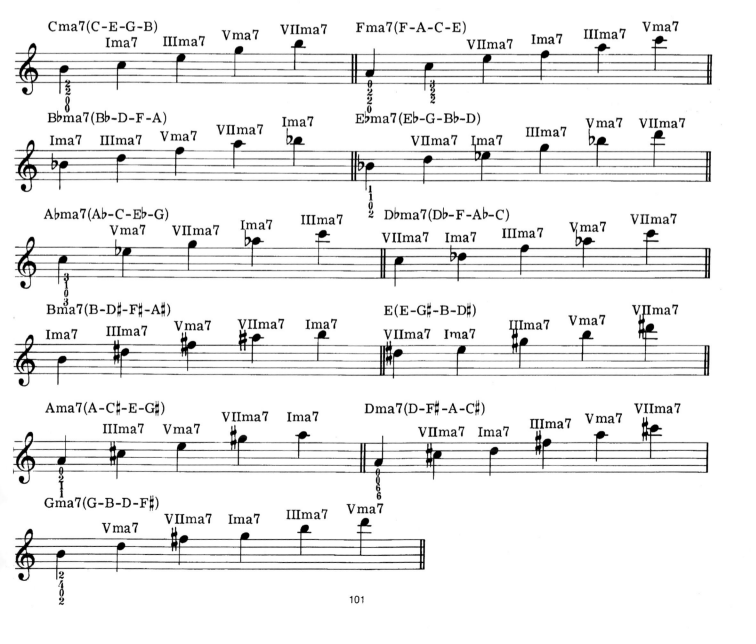

A Major-Seventh Chord Etude

When using the major-seventh chord in progressing from the I form of the major to the I7 form of the seventh, us the optional major and seventh forms.

A Major-Seventh Chord Etude

The Minor-Seventh Chords

Symbol = m7

The minor seventh chord is made by lowering the third of the dominant seventh chord.

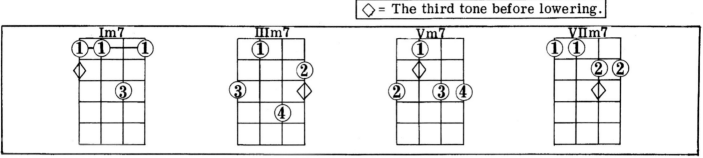

The Inversions

When going from the I7 to the Im7 form us   the optional I7 form

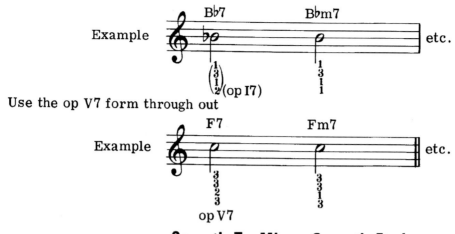

Use the op V7 form through out

Seventh To Minor-Seventh Etude

The Seventh Augmented-Fifth Chord

Symbol = 7+5

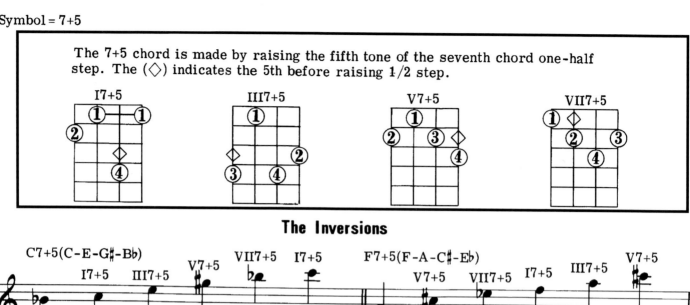

The Inversions

7th To 7+5 Etude

The Seventh Diminished-Fifth Chord

Symbol = 7-5

The 7-5 chord is made by lowering tone of the seventh chord 1/2 step.

The (◊) indicates the fifth before lowering.

THE REASON FOR THE MANY DOUBLE-FLATS (♭♭) IN THE ABOVE INVERSIONS IS: THE CHORD-SPELLING NEVER CHANGES.

The Ninth Chords

Symbol = 9

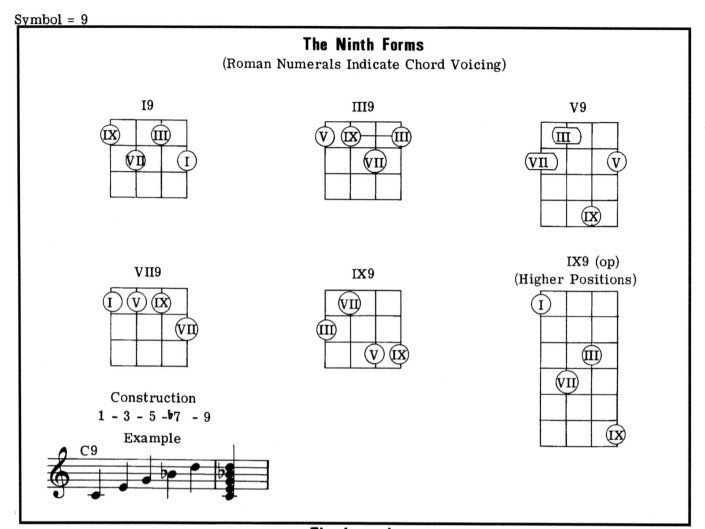

The Inversions

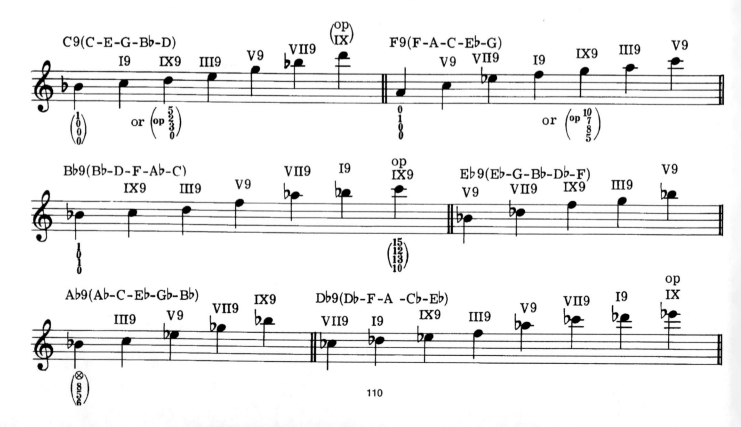

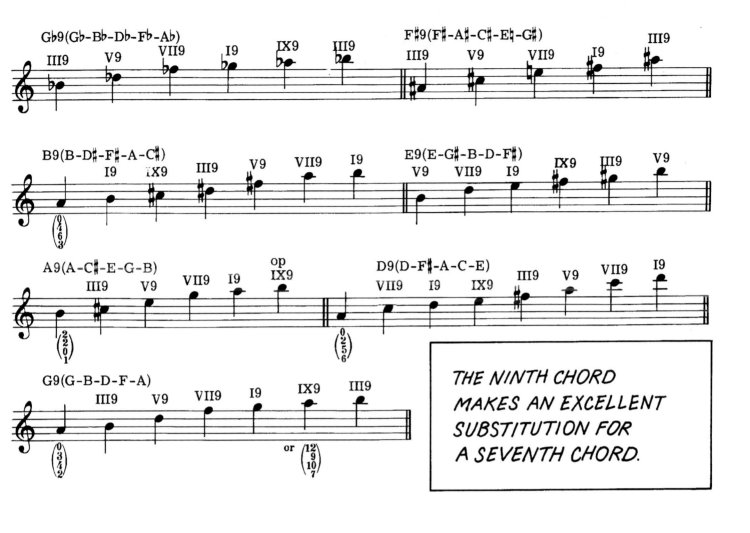

THE NINTH CHORD MAKES AN EXCELLENT SUBSTITUTION FOR A SEVENTH CHORD.

7th To 9th Etude

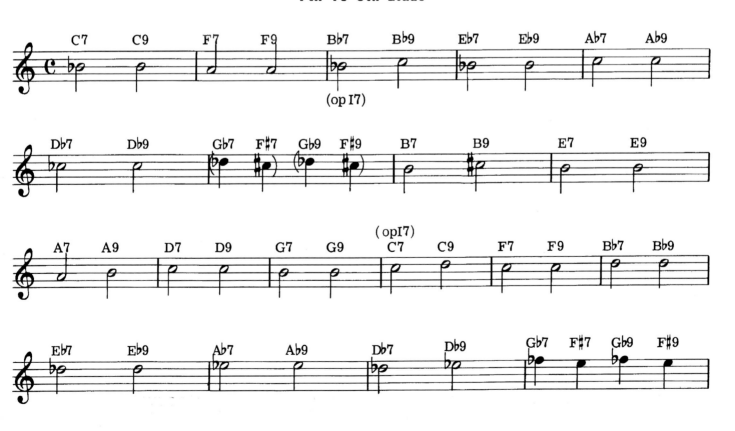

The Ninth Chord Intervals

I = Root   III = 3rd   V = 5th   VII = 7th   IX = 9th

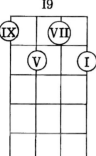 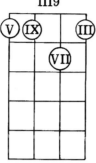 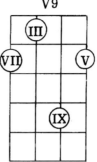 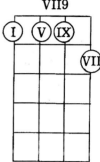

The Altered Ninth Chords

Mi9 = Lower (III) 1/2 Step

9+5 = Raise (V) 1/2 Step

9-5 = Lower (V) 1/2 Step

Ma9 = Raise (VII) 1/2 Step

-9 = Lower (IX) 1/2 Step

+9 = Raise (IX) 1/2 Step

Practice altering each ninth-chord chromatically up the finger board.

PLAY THROUGH THE CIRCLE OF KEYS.

𝄞 C C9 CMi9 | F9 | F Mi9   Throughout the etude.

𝄞 C C9 C9+5 | F9 | F9+5   "   "   "

𝄞 C C9 C9-5 | F9 | F9-5   "   "   "

𝄞 C Cma9 Fma9 | B♭ma9 E♭ma9   "   "   "

The Augmented Ninth Chord

Symbol (9+)

Raise the (IX) 1/2 Step

◇ = 9th before raising. Repeat the etude on page and play first the ninth chord followed by the altered chord.

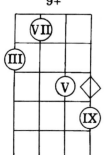

113

The 11th Chords

Symbol = 11th
(Some times called a 7sus4 or 9sus4

◇ = Third(3rd)

By raising the 3rd 1/2-step (to the 4th) in a 7th or 9th chord you produce an eleventh chord in the following forms the 3rd is indicated by the (◇).

Due to the fact that the Tenor-Banjo is a four stringed instrument, we will substitute the 7sus4 and 9sus4 chords instead of the eleventh chords.

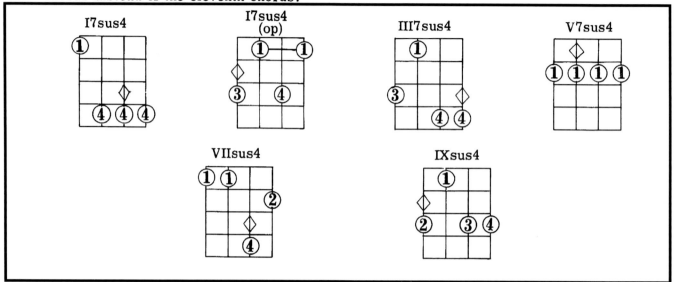

I7sus4 to I7 (op Form)

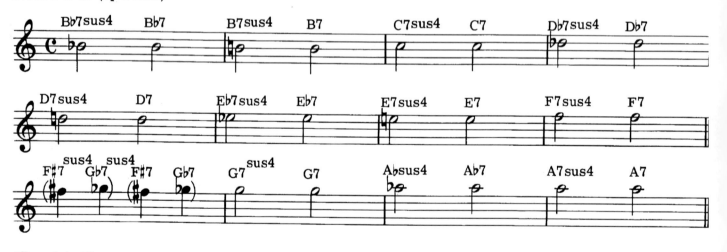

I7sus4 to I7

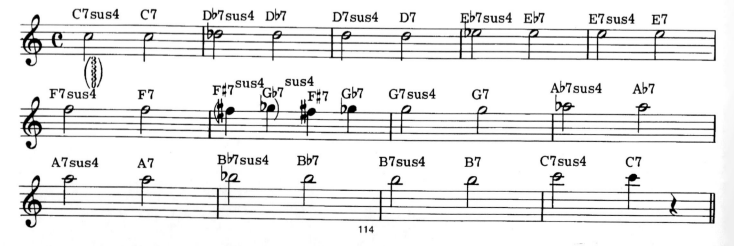

The Augmented-Eleventh

Symbol (11+)

This chord is made by raising the 11th 1/2 Step

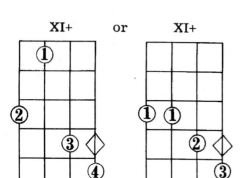

The Thirteenth Chords

(Sometimes referred as 7add6 or 9add6)

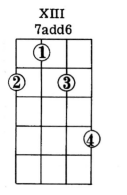
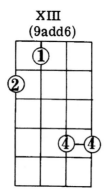
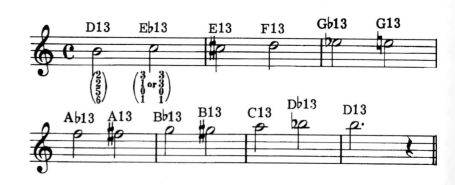

The Thirteenth Diminished Ninth Chord

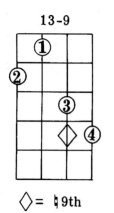

116